AN ENGLISH APOCALYPSE

Books by George Szirtes

George Szirtes

AN ENGLISH APOCALYPSE

BLOODAXE BOOKS

ISBN: 1 85224 574 3

First published 2001 by
Bloodaxe Books Ltd,
Highgreen,
Tarset,
Northumberland NE48 1RP.

Bloodaxe Books Ltd acknowledges
the financial assistance of Northern Arts.

Cover printing by J. Thomson Colour Printers Ltd, Glasgow.

Printed in Great Britain by
Cromwell Press Ltd, Trowbridge, Wiltshire.

for Thomas and Helen
born here in England

ACKNOWLEDGEMENTS

Acknowledgements are due to the editors of the following publications in which some of the new poems in the second section of this book first appeared: *Birdsuit, Critical Quarterly, The Dublin Review, European Judaism, The Forward Book of Poetry 2000* (Forward Publishing, 1999), *Hudson Review* (USA), *The Irish Times, Metre, The New Exeter Book of Riddles* (Enitharmon Press, 1999), *New Writing 8* (Vintage, 1999), *Poetry Review, The Review* (USA), *The Rialto, Salisbury Review, The Times Literary Supplement* and *The Waterlog*.

'Backwaters: Norfolk Fields' was shortlisted for the Forward Prize for Best Individual Poem in 1999.

Some of the poems were read and discussed on *Work in Progress* (BBC Radio 3).

The earlier English poems in the first section were first collected in these books: *Poetry Introduction 4* (Faber & Faber, 1978); *The Slant Door* (1979), *November and May* (1981), *Short Wave* (1984) and *The Photographer in Winter* (1986), published by Secker & Warburg; and *Metro* (1988), *Bridge Passages* (1991), *Blind Field* (1994), *Selected Poems 1976-1996* (1996) and *Portrait of My Father in an English Landscape* (1998), published by Oxford University Press.

I am indebted to Trinity College Dublin and The British Council who enabled me spend a terms as International Writer Fellow at TCD, where most of the *English Apocalypse* sequence was written.

G.Sz.

CONTENTS

An English Apocalypse

PREFACE

England: a rough grey blanket, tea, the sea in winter, Tommy Steele singing *What a marf*, cliff edge, scout hut, bus spotting, football in baggy shorts, red maps, red buses, the swelling pillow of the London suburbs. The list could go on. I remember when all these things seemed strange and new, and in a sense they have remained so.

The major psychological turning point in 20th-century English history is arguably Suez, and my family arrived from Hungary on the very crest of it in the December of 1956. Having cast ourselves away in our new country we rose and fell with its tides. I recall the stroke of new year in 1960 when I was 11, thinking that something significant would surely happen at a change of decades. We had moved around north London in our first few years, passing from rooms and maisonettes to little terrace houses and eventually a semi-detached. My mother loved it: loved the gardens, the tree-lined streets, the parks, the privacy, the mild political ambience of the Butskellite consensus and the gadget-equipped, G-Plan-furnished, Raphael Soyer-decorated home comforts that seemed to make up for years of terror and anxiety in concentration camps and bomb-shattered apartment blocks, under paranoid régimes, enduring Warsaw Pact shortages. Unfortunately she was ill and getting worse. Eventually the upward graph of happiness met the downward graph of misery and started falling with it. It was a kind of learning process.

Like the rest of my family, like all other refugees and immigrants, I was learning England. England was a safe landing, a virgin harbour protected by an unbreachable sea wall and the RAF. It was one of history's winners. It was a privilege to be *Made in England*. It was even welcoming in its slightly grey, rough, damp, icy-sheeted way: we were after all regarded as potentially heroic figures. Icy sheets equalled Cold War. But it was warming up. English words, Anglo-American words, had begun to seep into me at school without me even realising it. I began to play with them, and ached with a kind of desire for their powers and colours. I was disorientated and grateful, hot and bothered. By the time I reached 20 at the end of 1968, I had started to write poems as though they were the most important things in the world. I read in an incoherent, chaotic way. My parents voted Labour throughout the 60s, vaguely horrified at what was happening to the world, and I, as an adolescent was riding the crest of significant changes: just too young to be at, say, Grosvenor Square, but old enough to feel breath of the 60s wafting me into art college.

England was not a conscious point of reference for me then, let alone a subject for poetry. I had arrived in the England of Betjeman and Larkin just as it was becoming the haunted and sometimes bloody ghostscape of James Fenton and Peter Reading. There was little I could intervene in there. I needed to start further back, further removed, in the visual arts. There was, I found, a deep, oddly exotic attraction in pictured pastorals such as I myself never painted, in the worlds of George Stubbs and Birkett Foster, which, I now think, served as instinctive personal metaphors for England. England, for me, for all of us, was the place where Nature, and by extension, the World, grew cultivated and inhabited: however despoiled it might have become, it embodied a gentle but imperial dream of enlightened subduing.

The appearance of such subjects in my earlier poems may have been no more than an echo of my parents' pleasure at the sight of front and back gardens, and their delight in an altogether fresh notion of privacy (call it diffidence, call it reserve) so different from the city we had grown up in. From the pure pastoral it extended out to 18th and 19th century genre painting: from Devis and Hogarth through to Wilkie and the mid-Victorians. I realise how dry and academic this might appear to others, to those who want the immediacy of life itself, but for me it was a way of entering a world as if by stealth. Looking back it seems to me that my early poems, however stilted and occasionally frozen they appeared, were that way because they were in some sense the working through of dreams with real loved and vulnerable people at the core.

These dreamlike poems, frozen because they so often dealt with frozen images from a frozen time, would seem no more than interesting examples of pathology, even to me, were it not that the world to which they provided an antithesis felt so dangerous and close. The fascination with Stubbs particularly was perhaps to do with sensing the power of the horses and the fragile code that held those horses in place. The frozen dreams of pastoral appealed precisely because of their fragility. At the centre lay a promise of human warmth: at their edges raged the uncontrolled. The island and the sea make a reasonable analogy for this.

I entered the England of imagination through the visual arts, but I was living in a practical, physical and political world which exerted its own pressure on the psyche. I don't know, nor do I even want to know precisely what it is I feel for England. Jo Shapcott, in her version of Tsvetaeva's 'Motherland' says what she feels is distance. That's not the way it was or is with me. Perhaps because

I am from elsewhere my feelings seem to me powerful, close and mixed. There is something about England that I love, and need to love, passionately and unconditionally, but I don't know what it is: the land? the people? the state? its institutions? These ideas are too general. Let it be then. Let the psychoanalysts discover a name and location for such feelings. But when they do so they should remember that there is also a degree of horror and even indifference tangled up with them. The poems in the sequence that give this book its name, *An English Apocalypse*, were mostly written in Ireland in the autumn and winter of 2000. They began as a small group of pastorals in the form of Dante's terza rima, then began to spin off in what seemed to me overwhelming but various directions. At the end of the poem England is destroyed by five apocalypses that spring out of a knot of feelings and apprehensions I could not begin to unwind. Some of them make me laugh, some frighten me.

Perhaps it is only because some fragile thing is at the core of the pastoral that I care for it so much. I suspect it may be to do with the delicacy of the ankles of the beautiful enormous horses in Stubbs's paintings and the isolation of the poor blank-faced grooms that attend on them. The land these 'English' poems offer may not be one fit for heroes, but I would like it to be fit for the grooms and the horses. The figure who meant most to me when I was younger was Blake: his burning energetic forms are, I think, the product of a troubled passion and a firm belief in the potential of the human imagination. Odd perhaps to think of Stubbs and Blake, the two great contemporaries, springing from the same soil.

I wanted in this book to present some fragments of a historical process as written over a historical period. My Hungarian selection *The Budapest File* (2000) dealt with the history of Hungary in roughly chronological fashion: An English Apocalypse is more like a temperature chart. The poems in the beginning were written in or near London, but the Apocalypse takes in Yorkshire and ends in the East of England where I now live, and where the deluge described in the last section begins.

GEORGE SZIRTES

12

EARLY ENGLISH

poems from earlier collections

Lilac, Laylock

1 *Lilac*

Early morning the lilac
quivered, threw out a track
of fragrance to the street,
pervasive, watery-sweet.

The choreography of water,
the drift of scent caught at,
swirling away, blown back,
was the cunning of the lilac.

She bristled sweetness, arched
like a girl. A bullfinch perched
on her crown, immaculate
in his feathers. His weight

bothered the lilac, she bent
a little, her small tent
of pleasure collapsing
inward with the swaying.

2 *Laylock*

The last place before sleep
in the changing cave;
the children rush to play
rolling on wild grass.

Black cherries fatten us
as we run down the hill.
The flies sleep in the bowl
among the newspapers.

The children dream. They run
towards us bearing faces
that are pinned out like rags
against the lilac branches.

No smell, though garden flowers
are in full bloom
and the queen wasp hovers
about the door.

The Child I Never Was

The child I never was could show you bones
that are pure England. All his metaphors
are drawn from water. His ears admit the sea
even to locked rooms with massive doors.

Look, let me make him for you: comb his hair
with Venus comb, a wicked drupe for mouth,
twin abalone ears, sharp auger teeth,
an open scalloped lung, a nautilus
for codpiece, cowrie knuckles, nacreous.
Let him shiver for you in the air.

The English schoolboy cannot understand
a country that is set in seas of land.

The child I never was makes poetry
of memories of landscape haunted by sea.
He stands in an attic and shows you his collection
of huge shells, and with an air of introspection
cracks his knuckle bones.

Sap Green: Old School

The copper dome of the old school had turned
into the colour of soup they used to serve
on certain Fridays. The dining-hall lights burned,
low in the autumn gloom, You boys deserve

all you get, muttered the head into his gown.
A desperate smell of tobacco. The old man
had a bad smoker's cough, his fingers brown
with age and decay, faintly reptilian.

Retreating backwards into the fog, the class
of '65 were entering the pool
of memory through dark translucent glass
the colour of sap. It was time's own school,

uniforms languishing in cloakroom showers;
the loss, the charm of wasted after hours.

Salt

It begins in salt, a pinch of white
added to a mound on a tablecloth
in a friendless boarding-house, where she talks
of striptease and he looks vaguely embarrassed,
makes sucking noises with his mouth,
and hates the elaborately curtained and terraced
six-room establishment with its 60-watt light
and its proximity to coastal walks.

It begins here, eating out the centre
of the past, an indifferent turning-away,
leaving an ache for the vanished
that goes on vanishing, eroding under
wind and sea, an ancient fishlike bay,
a resort that ages badly and turns blander
with each year that heads for winter,
and still the story isn't finished.

Sealed tobacco tins and open drawers
of pale devices, magazines that burn
in hands, the smell of adult beds.
A lit room in a window, the reflection
of a boy writhing like a worm,
the black panes each with its clear section
of interior, of walls and doors
that bear the familiar burdens of his head.

This was the parental home the sea
brought in, its end in its beginning
tail-in-mouth eternally. This cold
and even light that levels out the tones
of summer autumn winter and the spring
within a narrow harmony of bones
and fossils will lend domesticity
to secret lives. And now they can be told.

Bodies

A brawny driver with enormous hands
is injured in an accident. At night
he shows his scar. His wife looks frail
as she describes the junction and the dark
where it all happened. Her eyes are bright,
dilate with impact, her shadow stark.
She begins to dance beside him where he stands –
immense, protective, vastly out of scale.

It is hard to know just where to place a thing.
A paper tissue blown against
a branch, the sea's seminal calm
shoving and caving. On the long settee
a couple smooches; a blonde-rinsed
girl, the man moustached and military
like a conjuror. They cling
together swaying palm to palm.

Every night a new performance.
Every night a new forging of links.
There's something in it quite methodical
and rather less than modest.
He wonders what the heavy driver thinks,
and what that frailness looks like when undressed,
what insinuations make palms dance
and how such largeness must be magical.

Like broken glass, the sea-spray
splinters, leaves her bodywork, her slap
of brakes. All couples are accidents,
mothers and fathers, bathers on the beach
among the towels in which they wrap
their changing bodies. They will teach
their children modesty. Their flesh is clay,
and kneadable. It smells of innocence.

Mr Reason

Dear Mr Reason, hook-nosed and Punch-jawed,
is nevertheless handsome and a hero
to the class of ten-year-olds who love to hear
his voice expand like an enormous football.
He is the ultimate inflated zero
of their short experience. Sometimes he'll call
on God in accents mild or cry him abroad
with trumpetry. He is their Chanticleer

and Unicorn. But now, hair powdered
by the blue dusk falling through the glass, he seems
an angel of some sort. The milk they hold
in their soft hands is what is drunk in heaven.
He speaks their names and summons them through dreams
of being good – Nigel, Sarvin, Trevor,
Jimmy, Wendy – tripping light-padded
among their words, gathering in his fold.

St Catherine's Lighthouse, Alum Bay, the Castle
where the king once slept. This miniature
isle of brightness is the heart of something
so indigenous it drags at small hearts
with reminiscences of furniture
in old men's rooms. There he too waits, a part
of sunlight, dusk, the seashore and the puzzle
of archaic words and comfortable singing.

His terror too: once in the pavilion
the groundsman found a mess, a human mess,
quite foul and brown, no bigger than an egg.
His furious inquest made them all ashamed.
But now well-being, warmth and doziness
creep over children pleased with being named
in Mr Reason's grace. Next afternoon
they'll hear a sermon by the Reverend Legge.

Acclimatisation

One minded one's manners those days. The fork
turned discreetly downwards, raking and spearing,
and chewing with mouth closed, despite mischievous
hints to the contrary. England was a cloud under
which one learned the dangers of interfering
in other people's business. A distant thunder
strung the roofs together as if by metalwork
and teachers in schools tried terribly to forgive us

our trespasses. We worried away at the lawn
like blind men learning the alphabet, listened
to the grave consensus of Butskellite heads
sprouting from their collars, took energetic
part in quiz-games where ladies glistened
in sequin and varnish, heard frenetic
voices by wrecked aeroplanes in a cold dawn
huddling in frozen grey-blanketed beds.

We also misheard: *puncher* for *puncture*,
wicked for *wicket*. They were comical times,
learning fixations and the twelve times table,
the inordinate lengths short trousers could go to,
the proper droop for socks, the sound of door chimes,
the hell-hole of pet shops. Sometimes we were slow to
pick up a hint, to smile at the appropriate juncture
of a given conversation, were too often liable

to solecisms of an almost terminal sort.
But God and our teachers forgave us. Meanwhile there were
the consolations of Ealing comedies,
the *Daily Herald* and all that wonderful Britishness
to keep us going. My mother drank her
black coffee with mountains of cream. We grew less
strange by the month. The days grew short
as did our affections. Soon we were anybody's.

Miss Pickering

Miss Pickering, like a pickled walnut,
dithered among palettes, swam in a haze
of thin spittle, shrank behind glass
till she attained a precious quality.
She coaxed and rutted tiny words of praise,
A very nice thing, dear and *Oh how pretty!*
and her pearly eyes opened and shut
on the big room and swallowed up the class.

They would, if they could, have learned from her
some grace or delicacy, but colours ran
in grey pools over scored lines
that represented nothing and were graceless.
Their hands remained stubbornly simian.
They dreamed of running fingers over a dress
or exploring the intricacies of long hair
through endless and romantic lunchtimes.

The girls themselves were consciously superior.
Their bodies moved beyond Miss Pickering
answering questions she would never ask.
They'd take from her as much of delicacy
as they required, then pass on, leave her twittering
about the small bones of a leaf, or the lacy
complications of flowers. They saw much clearer
the powers around them and took larger risks.

I think of Miss Pickering dead, a needle in
the darkest of haystacks, of filigree,
of egg and dart, of finial and crocket
and the worrying precisions of needlepoint
like white foam stitched to the borders of the sea
riding its back astride the slopping paint.
It's something, after all, to sidle in
and keep a little in so small a pocket.

Seaside Postcard

The sea contracted to a water pistol
is pointed at a child's head and explodes
in laughter. It is autumn. Leaves litter
the pavements. Dry, they are as delicate
as dead skin. Even the wet roads
ignite under our feet and store the late
weak sun till evening comes. A dark pastel
obliterates them all. The nights are bitter

as fine chocolate and as sweet. The games
continue in and out of private gardens,
round fat public trees. Manners grow stiff
at neighbours' open gates. The scout huts beckon
their lost hearties: small boys, churchmen, wardens.
Front rooms fill with TV. The American
comics dance across the screen, trail names
of power through grey and white in low relief.

The child appears, wide-eyed as an icon,
learning the words, staring at a space
beyond the inner one of Now. He wears a comic
pullover, hair parted in horns of light.
The wind is striking at his open face,
gets in among the teeth. The sea is white
against the rows of houses, waves break on
walls and grey-green tide marks stain the brick.

The situation has been well prepared,
preserved in frozen worlds of *Beezers*, *Toppers*,
Beanos and *Dandys*. A dog leaps from a gate
with sharp teeth snapping, worrying at his heels.
The words have gathered in his heart like coppers
which can be spent now, freely. He appeals
for help, his hands extended, running scared.
His yell is comic and articulate.

North Wembley

The mongol boy makes friends over the fence,
his cat owns all the local mice.
From hosepipes squirts the Sunday carwash.
Tom and Joan are decorating.

There are trees, grass verges, a parking space,
and alleyways, alleyways by the dozen.
Khan is arguing with his wife.
The train whistles through an empty station.
Blackberries by the railway are quickly stripped.
Jewish boys practise the violin in dark but modern lounges.

Over the main road there is a Sporting Club
with pitches stretching out to distant hedges
from where, one summer night, a lazy rat
emerged and crossed, legally, over the zebra.

At Table, 1964

At Schmidt's in Charlotte Street the old waiter
scuttled between tables, wrinkled as Adenauer.
The menu was opulent, the covers clean.
We ate wiener schnitzel with potatoes and sauer-
kraut chased by crème caramel, our table talk
joky-familiar or sour. We were creatures of mood,
and Sunday a family occasion, like bridge
or *Monopoly*, was a debt owed to childhood,
keeping track of lost time.

And lost time is what the restaurant suggested
with figures in shadows and rooms beyond rooms.
I can still taste the food in that arrested
development, the breadcrumbs rough on my lips,
and I find myself rattling on, as if I were an old waiter,
finding the whole thing funny and boring and sad.

That is the beauty of it: the poetry comes later,
shuffling up to you like a Low Church sacrament,
a grey-suited man with non-alcoholic wine,
glass concentrated in a bead of dark red,
serving for sign.

The Past Order

We reach back into some past order
to reshuffle the pack, coming up
with ancient medallions till now kept
stored away. He who was once King
is reduced to plotting minister,
the greenwood is repopulated
with silver fruits that droop precipitously
from the branches, falling
every so often with a soft sound
that stifles the screaming of mice.

News for Signor Mouse

Who is dead? Who? Who?
Signor Mouse will tell
the kitchen sink of this,
and those bare floors will
stink of disinfectant;
propitiatory; the incense of Paradiso.

One is dead, and two are dead,
now three. Whispers
at the perimeter, closer still
and closer, tickling the thick-skinned grass
from underneath;

faces cut in mid-sentence:
Signor Mouse, hurry –
tell the cat of this.

Group Portrait With Pets

The little group seems perfectly at ease
though drapes and scattered toys confirm the truth,
it was the clever painter's artifice
that fixed the glimmer on each eye and tooth.

I say there will be hopelessness before
the children rise and the chair topples back:
the bright, transparent skins will fold and crack
before the painter leaves by the back door.

That satin, crinoline, so much like blood
splashed across the canvas, find an echo
in the bird's breast, the cat has understood
who simply bides his time while others go,
who has seen terror written on a face
just as the limb is torn and the claw sinks.

The artist too, in spite of what he thinks,
can only measure breath in a small space,
where husbands, wives and children interlink
and find a warmth in the arranged embrace.

Masters

Black and gold, a kiss upon the muzzle,
then a rod, taut paxwax, technicalities –
a blasted tree that leans before the sea and grass,
grooms mounted and prancing, tantivy and heel!
Always work to be done but unobtrusively
with a fistful of hay or the stiff brush
or a neat pair of shears.

They ride smoothly in a rising arc
obedient to the rod and time of day,
each masked horse hides an identity and rhythm
firm behind its cloth, the vaguer dogs
are lost to their precision:
a head protruding from the bush
gives a name to reticence.

And O how fine their masters are
whose eyes observe in classical allusions
the shades of Watt and Newton tracing Ceres
across acres of wheat; they laugh in caesuras
and sharpen ankles till they are like glass
but when they break there is no mending them;
the horses will be very sorry for this.

At Colwick Park

First thing in the morning they went out
to rake over the lawn. The horses
waited quietly in their stalls, snuffling
at wet latches. Birds were already singing
behind the roof; dull blades rusted
in drops of condensation. While others were asleep
they worked, sowing their own bodies in Colwick Park.

Their aprons sweep them round. Rakes to earth,
certain of their footing, they stare
across the field of their flesh
with no apparent emotion. A sharpness comes
to peel away their noses but they counter it

with work: Swish, swish of hewn wood descending.
Recoil of grass, resilient in clouds
of green; the regular clicking of arms.

Clouds can only echo their shapes.
The stubble was dragged clear, the lawns
levelled without anger. Their sullen staring
is what is left when mythologies disappear.

Rest on the Hunt

Riders cascade down the valley in the
wrong direction. Here the chase is over
and the dogs relax, chewing, wading
in the ditch and rolling about. The horses
twist their heads uncomfortably. They
are not at ease. The brush has been
detached, examined and is now hung
from the saddle. No one looks at it.
The master seeks further game and waits
for pursuers to wheel his way. How sharp
is this air: the explosion into death
has left a tang. They savour it
and remain stock still, bitten by the acid
into a climax from which all movement would be decay.

Romantic Episode

They are remote, polishing their rifles
in a boskage. The trees are magical,
they magnetise the soil. Hush, hush, attend!
As the rabbit pops from the undergrowth
two barrels gleam simultaneously,
then the rabbit disappears, tail flicking,
before their report. There will be more along.
Down goes the ramrod and the flintlock snaps back.
The forest is their down, their bed of feathers
and has been so since before Merlin's time,
but it is dark here, dark and melancholy,
and the dog whines quietly to himself.
It isn't long then till the hedges part
and a beast far greater than their expectation
causes them to flee in self-defence,
still jovial and priggish, to their horses
(who have long lean bodies and death's heads)
prancing at the skirt of the trees.
The groom is sagging slightly at the buttocks.
The horses laugh at them, are kept in trim...

Pastoral

The ancient at the gate wickers a chair:
bald-headed, hunched, he is focus
for a metropolis of ants while on the bank
stubble grows aggressive. He is an English Joseph
earning pin-money. Behind him
in the topmost room the god-child slumbers
as the child-wife sings over the oven,
the neighbour's children brawl in the sun
(one's watching him now as he turns away)
and the trees fling their doily patterns high.

No doubt a flock lathers in the valley,
no doubt an owl stirs in the hayloft,
no doubt the spider bridges its rafters:
there are laws and ordinances, local rites,
to say nothing of precedents to be observed.

In the quarry feet start a stampede of stones
and the wind is heard by listeners in the hedge.
The gammer starts a story though the children know the ending.

Sheep-shearing at Ayot St Lawrence

The muzzle firmly held between his knees
he gathers the fleeced stomach into pleats
and leans forward across the flaccid belly
to push the razor down towards her teats.

And there she sits, blind-mouthed, flat on her rump,
black-legged on a sheet of polythene
like some old woman at the hairdresser:
she's corpulent and yellow and unclean.

Behind her stands a cottage with a garden
where a real old woman serves out pots of tea,
and further back the church, Palladian,
which acts this Sunday as a gallery.

Someone at the door sells raffle tickets,
the catalogues are handy on his desk:
inside the close-hung paintings testify
to the attractions of the picturesque.

The sun is out, the summer heat is stifling,
pouring across smooth shoulders, washing hands,
a clean, hard light cuts definitive shadows.
The man relaxes, lets her drop, and stands

above her with a needle, plunges in.
The anxious lambs are nudging underneath
their unshorn dams. It is an ideal moment.
The ewe escapes. Sheep stud the hill like teeth.

Village Politicians
(after Wilkie)

Their heads are too big for a start. Their bodies
shrink to pup-like cowering, all hunched.
Gestures are means of voiding the bowels; air reeks
in the small room where they are bunched

around the table in endless argument.
A frenzy grips them surely! Faces fall
to ape Michelangelo's *Damnation*, a small boy
steals the dog's dinner, woodlice crawl

out of the rotting beams, and a carving knife
lies on the floor among the debaters who
are growing angry. The fireplace is threatened
by encroaching darkness. Time fixes them like glue.

The Birdcage 1851

She leans to kiss the cage in the full sunlight
of the conservatory doorway. Walls gleam
down the shade-patched drive, a pair of pigeons, alight
on the apple tree. Everything is stiff as a dream,

and so she strains to the bird's mouth that draws her up,
stretching out her neck – though she could scarcely approve
this sensual exhibition, nor the cup
that tilts to spilling from her hand as she moves –

and draws her hands and breasts up and shuts her eyes...
The sleeping dog crumpled at her feet
stirs a paw to wave away some flies:
wings buzz interminably in the heat.

The glass is vibrant with its rainbows; flowerpots
perched sullenly on the rough sill glow brick-red.
The bird's small feet are sharp and her beak cuts
the pouted fruitage of the lady's head.

At the Circus

No need to ask what the black horse is,
or the dripping tinsel tickling Mamie's hair,
as she perched delicately on her husband's knee,
courses spirals through the blurring air.

Round and round we go the children cry,
next to their respectable papas;
the red-tongued horse invites their crisp applause,
the ringmaster hands round immense cigars.

We fill the sagging tent and pay no heed
to the tin clowns clattering across
the sawdust. The grey air above us bleeds,
the lollipops are cold, voluptuous.

Three Dreams

1

The yellow rusting of the late apples under the trees:
insects to lunch. We are almost dead – ancient localities

stuck in intricate plumbing of decay. Almost dead
almost dead, old masters. Bestuccoed in white lead

we flake off bark or blade, struggling for breath, running
in autumn rain. We watch the young girls swing

pendulums into the park's throat – it is we who choke,
go down with flags flying into the still lake.

2

Except you. You don't come down this way – I'm glad.
The marshes croak: I find my place in the *Dunciad*

with Crousaz and Burgersdyck. Everyone else wins
plaudits; I'm overwhelmed by my stripling sons...

3

Words revolt against the weak king. Effeminate, he
is condemned to be locked into a shelf of his library

between the first two volumes of Mickey Mouse. Castrati
lull him to sleep but he's woken at night by the noise of parties

on a lower floor. A heavy fog descends:
the autumn brings pear-falls in the garden.

Two Men in a Boat

(i.m. L.S. Lowry)

Are rowing in opposite directions.
Their names are Sid and someone
and they are stuck somewhere in the middle
of a boating lake where ice-cold gulls
lever themselves off a pack of houses.

The boat is rain and tastes of
old tobacco. Reflected in
the water, two swans
do not like each other
and attempt to pull away.

In the dark leaves of the umbrella plant
a man with a lute, a nun with a dirty habit,
and the sea-scum laughing with its bones askew,
and these two seem to be singing to each other
about the weather and the lake,

or Lear's oddikins, those dear men,
rushing round in a sieve,
whirlpool against whirlpool.
At least they are enjoying themselves
though the songs are sad,

because it's kisses they bestow
on one another in the yellow light,
like Siamese twins growing out
of each other's skulls,
away from each other. And the boat will break

with a loud guffaw, brother Lawrence,
and the oars slam at nothing
but winter and winter's comforts,
hollow trees shouting at one another
across the waves.

The Claude Glass

A tiny house. The tiny couple move
with the huff and delicacy of birds.
He has the best room and finest view
while she keeps company beside the fire,
brother, sister and all the children
shrunk to a Dutch peepshow, a Claude glass.
The weather holds, a lean boy drives the cows
down to the lake from where the view is striking,
hills and crags bareback on one another
and the house still tinier, still shrinking.

Through the window of a rented farmhouse
I see my wife and children moving dumbly
through a history made picturesque.
In their peepshow all is a pearl stillness,
a singing place for eyes and teeth,
a box to keep absorptions locked away.
The sharp cat is fixed against the floor.
Through the glass you may contemplate the sun's face.

The Silver Tree

In a hot steamed up room five girls are spinning
a tree made of silver paper, growing
from a trunk so clumsy only a child
could be taken in by it. Its girth outstrips
the attenuated branches that tumble
from its crown and drop down to the floor where
they coil and lengthen, lovelier than hair,
a genuine silver tree they seem to spin
out of themselves. Their fingers diminish,
twine with foil, are sucked out of their sleeves.
It is the triumph of Aluminium.

And just as they become the tree, the tree
becomes them. They thrive on ambiguity.
As the tree grows they grow, although
infinitely more slowly, and enter into
the frieze where mothers and smart daughters dance
in a cold pastoral. Ice is eating them.

It is desire for perpetuity,
the film rerunning as they petrify
and the forest throws its lank arms about them.
They hang like fruit, sucked out, perfect, until
imaginary gods pass by and cut them down.

Picnic

Two dogs are in love. The children seek
spiders in the scrub and place their hands
gingerly upon stalks, their mouths agape.

Their sisters and aunts pick flowers which they will
press between the leaves of poetry books
marking time if nothing else. Trees wash away
and the dogs' tails curl tighter. Rakish uncle
looks smug with his fair companions.

This is how order is made: the clipping down
of untidy edges, the finding of the spider.

A Walk Across Fields

(for Winifred Upchurch)

Not to have known the landscape was my loss –
a scoop of cloud held all the land, the sky
was panes of glass, and rain in quiet gutters
shook like leaves.

The streets for walking, rooms for dreams, the grass
in parks for small adventures: one could die
in forests, magic castles, doorways, broken shutters,
in urban graves

where books held all the secrets. Wind blows across
the river. The trees are bending. Thick clouds lie
like wadding on them. Distant predators
move in droves

beyond the bands of rain. The sleeping palace
wakes to potent thunder. The children dry
their clothes. I think of parents, grandmothers,
the natural loves.

Inuit

I have fallen in love with this baby
whose empty eyes and wrinkled mouth
appear to be essence of baby,
his death a perfect pathos
without sentiment, still as a photograph
of stillness, without potential energy,
with how he looks and does not look at me.

Could he be the Christchild under an Eskimo moon,
part moon himself with pitted eyes,
proverbial round cheese, a comforting thing
in uncomforting space, registering surprise
at the thingness of anything and everything?
And why is he more touching than any live baby?
More nocturnal, more animal? And might he wake up soon?

I hit a deer once, doing a steady lick
at dead of night. Its quivering body
was a thousand startled eyes. I didn't see him fall
but felt his dark soft leg, a heavy stick,
hammer briefly at my metal sheath
then disappear as we sped on, unable
to adjust to his appearance, or
the knowledge of his death.

It was on the brow of a hill. We were heading north,
the notional arctic, but would later bend east
toward Norfolk as the sky lightened. I want to speak light
for the baby, that he might understand. Let him at least
hear the noise of our passage over the earth
and watch the live deer crashing out of sight.

Preludes

1

All evening I kept running over leaves –
their small dry hands were spiders scurrying
until I broke them. They were in a panic,
some cataclysm might have overtaken
the whole leaf population as I started
down a B-road behind the motorway.
East Anglia, Home Counties, darkened twisters
of hills, punk hedges, sleek old villages
in lamplight, shops with lawnmowers and chainsaws,
the distant sky a television glow
between high trees. I thought: this is my prelude,
the beginnings of a gothick fantasy,
half-pulp, half-mysticism, school-of-Palmer,
the understatement of an English landscape
whose skin is tight and heavy, lumps of shine
receiving a faint covering of moonlight.

2

It wasn't like this in the soft green books
of Dickson Carr, Ngaio Marsh and Christie.
The libraries, the dens, the inglenooks
have only ghosts to fear,
though when you look the moon is far from clear
and the moor is slightly misty.

How can you take a murder seriously
when everyone's in costume? Bumbling inspectors
stage their re-enactments with mysteriously
poor results. Old cars
are found abandoned under field of stars
rusting away with harvesters and tractors.

A lack of motive, boredom, pressure, panic.
A television shivers into light
against an empty wall, with its babbling manic
insistence on being heard.
Whatever was going to happen has occurred
and is repeated hourly through the night.

3

A single man could creep out of the hills
and, moving purposefully, disappear.
A smell of petrol and an unlit car
on which the well-intentioned moonlight falls
with its mandate for restoring law and order.
The latest pastoral involves a murder.

Discarded anoraks, kagouls. The killer leaves
a trail of functional overgarments, camps
and boots, four empty tins from petrol pumps,
and, underneath the hedge, a pair of gloves,
reminders of the hands that broke from wrists,
a flaccid emptiness formed into fists.

Her hands, or someone's. As the leaves shake free
of barrel-loads of rain he sees her hands,
sole presences in stadiums, a stand
of favours, green and purple like the sea.
A pub winks in the distance. Music sweeps
across the fields: the damp grass bucks and dips.

He goes to ground and finds a hidden nickname –
Some rural creature, rat or mole or fox
which show him only their inhuman backs.
The earthworm fits him and invites him home
to supper where they share a piece of turf
and someone strangles him with his own scarf.

4

A lorry bent its head and seemed to graze,
a tall brick house backed on to CRODA GLUES
and the grass was rotting baize.
The fields of rape hummed at a ragged sky,
long strips of surgical tape were laid across
young lettuce. I watched the hulks of sleeping sheep emboss
a pasture, having dragged along the hedge
their trail of dirty candy floss.

A Pakistani read *The Yorkshire Mart*,
a headless windmill guarded British polder,
a shaft of sunlight opened like a guillotine,
and a white horse drank his own reflection
in a muddy field. Everywhere the green
retreated into dampness, growing colder
and colder, to a sub-zero diction
of bulletins that stirred my foreign heart.

A Greek Musée

When I look at my room I see powder. Life as a footnote
to unwritten literature. The chair with its thick varnish
picked up at a junk-shop, heading for a junk-shop,
is preparing, even now, to vanish.

A few thousand books gathering dust and amber
and half the books not read.
Literature is this torn old pair of slippers.
The plaster flakes and weals above my head

continually aspiring to the condition of literature,
the facets of a crystal. I listen to a record
knowing every voice on it is dead but breathes
volumes into my chaotic word-hoard.

I inhabit a communal Musée
des Beaux Arts where all things learn through error,
perfecting their falls from grace. I read the papers
for anthologies of terror.

And look, a shepherd watches a child fall
on to Greek soil, followed by the mother, followed
by a man's leg, followed it seems, by the sky.
Literature is Chicken Licken's fellow.

When I look at my room I see Greece. The bloody Gods
are resting on my two seater settee,
modelled on Habitat and falling to pieces now.
All will be patched up in God's new city,

all will be literature, as perfect as the armour
in the basement of the Fitzwilliam; the plates,
the pots, the pictures and samplers, and the drafts
of Auden, Spender, Tennyson and Yeats.

The Old Newspapers

I discovered Atlantis when I drowned.
It was a pleasant going down. My gutturals
were smoothed out as the sea rose higher
with all the colours of petrol.

Old warehouses of stuff from '51,
left over from the Festival of Britain,
faces from Ealing comedies, dead Sellers,
dead Hancock, a benign pattern

of cheerful decay. I heard the manic laugh
of Secombe and saw the exaggerated curve
of a girl's rump slipping behind the piano
crying, *I am what you deserve!*

(She squeezed her breasts to emphasise the point.)
Boxed gardens bristled with box and swam in a slough
of their own despond. Ducks, geese and chickens
would regularly plough

the soil to lead and silver. Up they drifted
and rose too, the dried kit of winter games,
flakes of dead grass, the smell of newspapers
with urgent crepuscular names:

the *Evening This and That*, the terraces
where headlines lost their vim, sodden
and mushrooming with fringed clouds in a cellar,
in a rhetoric forgotten

by Cassandras, Crossbenchers and Spot the Ball.
My face dissolves in print, a ticket
for the underground gone under.
I feel the weight of the pound in my pocket,

and know it to be the same, a green sea lettuce
wrinkling like a face, its lips pursed for the kiss
of fossilisation, knowing the softest leaf
must shrink and solidify to something like this.

Tinseltown

Nothing but a glittering you can't describe,
nothing but names and smiling at faces: no
jewels but plastic beads, no tiaras but card,
no face but that which fits you, a tall mirror
hung by the magazine rack, some pearls of frost
on the window beyond, dripping elegance,

full of December, and rain starting to dance
on the pavement where a woman has just crossed
this busy road to push through the double door
to where you stand by the counter, working hard,
totting money at the till in a green glow
of figures, servant to that commonplace tribe

queuing for papers though it's nothing to do
with you what the tabloids blaze across the front
page, you simply read it along with the rest
and it's good for a giggle, just like this crown
of tinsel you got wound into your hair, which
catches the lampglow all the way down the aisle

and slips occasionally forward, so while
you are counting you're always having to switch
hands and flick the thing back so it won't fall down,
but sits perky and sparkling, a silver nest
of light, frivolous, and when it falls you don't
stop to pick it up, it means nothing to you.

Gunsmith

All day the gas-jet glows in the gunsmith's window.
His long slow face is yellow with it. He smiles
like a shy man, even his moustache is shy.
Plainly he loves his work, he takes so much care with it.

Chiefly it's polishing, soothing, easing the barrel clean,
rubbing down abrasions, filing out a scratch,
straightening sights. He is making an object,
himself a part of the product of his skill.

Thoroughly gentle, almost apologetic,
how difficult it would be to dislike him
in his honest endeavour, his modest demeanour

as he turns the barrel over, blows hot dust away,
as he makes space for himself in the glow of his window,
in the soft detonations of light when somebody enters.

An Accident

You're simply sitting down. It's getting late.
The sky is a thick slab of premature dark,
metallic, of imponderable weight.
And noises start: a scratch, a whoosh, a bark.

Sometimes you read of accidents: a child
killed in a car, a freak wind raising hell
in an obscure American town, wild
storms of atoms raging inside a shell,

and it's like the room is just too full of you,
your senses, your own presence in the chair,
your breathing hands and feet, all pressing through
a visible integument of air.

I watch you sitting down as on a stage.
The accident begins. You turn the page.

*　*　*

Prayer for my Daughter

1

So here we are and here's my stanza,
like a Clementi cadenza
a penny-plain extravaganza,

just to keep things neat but sprightly
in what might otherwise politely
decline into a straight unsightly

father-to-daughter patronising
advisory misadvising
lecture on vague points arising,

a Yeatsian prayer to admonish
characteristics too Maud Gonneish,
Fenian or Amazonish.

2

My stanza's nineteenth-century capers
are out of time. I read the papers
and know the new opinion shapers,

I know their loose, sincere demotic
ironies and semiotic
quiddities, but I'm Quixotic:

though windmills are as quaint as giants,
I continue in defiance
of gravity or modern science

rhyming like a man demented
dolphin torn and gong tormented
till the giants have relented.

3

Darling, tonight the whole horizon
closed like a lid. The traffic sighs on
rainy tarmac, men flit like flies on

jets of wind, the river fractures,
and a streetlight manufactures
a wealth of frazzled broken textures.

So beautiful: the petrol station's
amber flatness, the quotations
of lit shopfronts, the impatience

of running clouds. The winter races
into darkness, interlaces
bodies in its breathing spaces.

4

You see, I want to turn this patter-
song to deeper, graver matter,
more throttle more carburettor.

I want to be a souped up, solemn,
portentous father, wise as Solom-
on not just a gossip column,

someone you'll take seriously
whose works you'll study furiously
not discard imperiously

from some theory-laden high-rise
nor swat and squash flat, wasp- or fly-wise
but approve, applaud and lionise.

5

Walking last night I sought an image
to offer you, a kind of homage
to the wind's wild scrape and scrimmage,

and noticed how the very cheapest
vulgarisms struck the deepest:
the Woolworth lights, a buckled leaf pressed

to the pavement, a crisp packet
flying in the gust. I took it
home with me, to store and stack it

in memory, imagination,
to use it in some combination:
a poem finding its occasion.

6

Some quick advice? Well just a quickie:
Beware the sentimental-sticky,
Beware the choosy and the picky,

Beware all those who talk in torrents
The snobs who earned the strict abhorrence
Of poor pale sickly D.H. Lawrence,

Beware the Oxfordly superior,
Beware those with a smooth exterior,
The cynic wiser and world-wearier,

Beware the shady and the murky,
Beware the overprecious-quirky,
Beware your father talking turkey.

7

Out on your own. The eighteenth hurdle
safely past. The tales I've heard all
tend to make a man's blood curdle,

so to the prayer (I'm feeling prayerful):
Darling be wise, be good, be careful,
be water, fire and earth and air-ful,

find images beyond the kitchen
that women used to bake and bitch in
from Halicarnassus to plain Hitchin,

may you, in darkness, be that changing
wind and light, your mind free-ranging,
sea-like, unplumbed, salt, estranging,

tender, yes, but not kid-gloving
neither too mousy, nor too shoving,
be fortunate, be loved, be loving

be all of these, be kind, far-seeing,
in short, beyond the you- and me-ing
all that befits a human being,

what human beings may be made for:
life, unearned, unknown, unpaid for,
that you were celebrated, prayed for.

* * *

AN ENGLISH APOCALYPSE

new poems

History

It was all so long ago that rain fell
antique yellow into the ornate gutters of the city.
Skirts were short or long, either way it was pretty,
and the whole world was frozen under the spell
of its own evanescence. I speak as a witness,
a napalm-scented ghost with a gift of flames
who even now can reel off sacred names,
the kind that glowed and terrified us witless.
I am an old soldier of the last empire, sold
into captivity by what then seemed eternal:
Brezhnev's beetling eyebrows, the sloping nose
of Tricky Dicky, bricks of South African gold.
I am an emperor, sans eyesight and sans kernel,
sans principles, sans annuity, sans clothes.

It was once upon a time, it was history,
it was the day before, the day that never happened.
The thing I am, or think I am, had ripened
to the semi-transparent spectre that you see.
True, there were consolations: when we held hands
or went driving, our hands in each other's laps,
but the car died like the other death-traps
and oil was creeping up deserted seaside sands.
People were blowing us up. The prime minister's lawn
was crowded with tanks. And as it is my dear,
I can't tell it straight, I don't think I would believe me.
It was the evening before the night before the dawn
and when we kissed we heard the ironic cheer
of what we thought was history mouthing *please don't leave me.*

I want a voice to speak this, twenty-nine
years of it, in a voice that is a hum heard down
telegraph wires from another, distant part of town,
or a train that is only a rumour mumbled on the line,
to tell us what is or was important, what made
time fly or the cat leap, or raised the alarm
about life passing with its dangerous feline charm,
morning, afternoon and night in a continuous parade
of light and darkness, blossoming and folding, you
in your girly skin, me in my own husk,
the years packed neatly away inside my purse
or so you'd think but always falling through,
the coins disappearing in the summer dusk,
my voice too straight, untuneful, strangely hoarse.

Time music is ghost music. The radio in the room
is speaking too quietly to hear so I turn it up.
It is us talking to each other across a narrow gap
at the beginning of the new millennium.
Like all human voices, we hang there a moment
as good as for ever, in a frozen frame
in a film made of frames, repeating the name
that holds us in its vague presentiment.
Those were our lips, and that noise we made
is still humming in the wires which are electric.
I am listening very carefully, my darling.
I am watching the dust swirling under the lampshade,
hoping to learn the odd useful evanescent trick
from the radio that fades a while then starts to sing.

Pearl Grey

Holding the egg was like trying to balance
light at the tip of your fingernail. It rose
almost weightless, a bubble born of chance
and sky at the point where creation froze
to one brief statement now about to crack.
There was a pair of earrings once, two pearls
in golden corollae gently peeled back
round hard glassy mist, nestling above curls
of hair. She might have been my mother, or
any other woman of a certain time
that now seems gone (though who can be that certain?)
There were clouds and scent of rain outside the door.
It was spring or summer, you could hear the chime
of ice-cream vans, the rustling of the curtain.

All time was concentrated in that egg
and life was delicate. Birds bustled in hedges,
slurring languages. One pecked at a clothes-peg,
another tugged at a worm at the edges
of vision. Time was simply the product
of flight and language. It was saying this
quietly to itself while waiting to self-destruct.
Light stood in a cup, too petrified to kiss
the draining-board. Everything stopped in fear.
My mother sat in the kitchen. I was elsewhere.
The ice-cream van was chiming. It was grey
outside, I remember. There, below her ear
hung the pendant or maybe it was hair.
The egg was slightly rocking on the tray.

The yellow dress my father fell in love with
(for Seamus Heaney)

It was the yellow dress my father fell
in love with: skimpy in late sixties style.

My father usually works till six. Meanwhile
the garden waits. The kitchen. The terrible
last years in the last house in the last street.
History has slipped off into the bushes where
it waits in darkness like a murderer.
The whole house has grown sticky and sweet.
He looks from the window, sees you at the end
of the garden and thinks: how beautiful.
He thinks you beautiful, as she once was
but gentler somehow as if you'd come to mend
his life or mine. And she is sitting at the table
where light is dancing as it always does.

VDU

The office seemed melancholy, as do all
offices. An elderly man fingered
sheets of paper, shadows crept under tall
filing cabinets, the typists lingered
over paper cups. I was between
school and college, an adolescent bard
vaguely attracted to the Ginsberg scene
about which I knew little. It was hard
being a prisoner of the old regime,
rubber stamping, envelope licking. True,
it was closer to home than jazz and Gregory Corso
but still I worked my mischief, in a dream
of late release and looked to being through
like everybody else there, only more so.

Later I was a visitor, a ghost
at the windows, catching sight of myself
superimposed on a view of streets, almost
transparent, as if across an immense gulf
between two worlds, one inside one out,
but did not recognise the figure at the desk
with its monitors, the man scuttling about
in the background, an impenetrable mask.
Most of the staff were still there, only more so,
gentler and kinder somehow and ageless,
this time with VDUs like goldfish bowls
to calm them. Each figure had a classical torso
clad in some version of Edward Hopper dress,
all of them faintly glowing like lost souls.

Like lost souls, only more so, only more lost,
and this was my fault, because almost certainly
it was I who'd lost them. An elderly man crossed
the room. It was my father, or a memory
of someone like my father. Or even me,
reflected in the glass on the other side
of the street. He sang. It was like hearing a tree
sing to the night which was coming in like a tide.
Soon the screens would be dark and the room
washed away. There'd be just one more black window
hiding the information it was meant to light.
Someone was moving in there with a broom,
tidying things though it was all too late and slow
to make much difference to anyone that night.

Triptych for Music

Dusty Springfield: My Brother's Wedding

Dusty Springfield singing, *I only wanna be with you*,
the sound of slippers flopping forward on the floor
and a little terrier at the bride's feet signifying, *faithful and true*.
The floorboards are bare and spotless, a fragile pallor

sits on their skins, an eggshell finish, and still Dusty sings
broken words in a broken voice: *Don't know what it is
that makes me love you so*. There are very few things
in the room: a mirror, a light-fitting, a few oddities

like fruit on the chest, a signature on the wall.
Everything points to the presence of a witness
in whose honour the bulb burns and the mirror reflects.

You've got to give me some of your loving... hours fall
into an empty cup, the years are clinging to her dress.
In the brilliant window-pane no dust collects.

Elvis 1956

They are playing *Heartbreak Hotel* on the juke box.
I am not quite eight years old but the *Ed Sullivan Show*
has let a monster loose on the world. The country rocks,
blue suede shoes tap. Here, in a drift of snow,

come the Russian tanks. My parents though
are listening to Franz Lehár and the Rákoczi March.
Their eyes are fixed on a beautiful merry widow
waltzing her way round the proscenium arch.

Today, Elvis is dead, but he winds himself up
to his full height. His legs begin to tremble
and his throat has that deep catch in it. My feet

move to the jive, following his. I can't stop
for the sheer drive of his voice and the simple
throb of a damp bass, as hollow as it's sweet.

Beautiful Place

Only one beautiful place, says music as it thrums
chords to itself. When I think of the beautiful place
I imagine it with Schubert. No one comes
and no one goes in the great organic palace,

everyone is alone. My parents are asleep
somewhere in the cellars, and the wind slips
through rooms several storeys deep.
I'm in the earth with them. Something grips

my heart. A violin is scribbling light
over the dark floor. These images are
pointless, I know. Music has no need

of what we say or think about it. Tonight
my mother is dead for the twenty-fifth year.
Schubert tiptoes through the house as I read.

The boys who beat up my brother
(for Andrew Szirtes)

1

The boys who beat up my brother, day after day,
had faces smeared with snot, their skin was grey.
They cornered him outside and raised their cry:
Jewboy, the name they knew my brother by.
Jewboy, *Jewboy*, they called him, and struck out.
Blows were the world they knew too much about.
And when that failed they told teacher who took
delight in hitting my brother with a book.

Blows were the world they knew. They could recite
the litany of those they had to fight.
The world was rough and little of it fair,
though you could ask it questions here and there.
But with no judge in chambers and no jury
rough justice called for pity or cold fury.

2

Cold fury is what I bring them. Every night
in their cold beds. Every morning over
breakfast. Every lunchtime. Every bite
they take. May they never again recover
their appetite or equilibrium.
It's late in the day, too late and much too late.
The furies that freeze outside have made the quantum
leap into ancient past as sheer dead weight.

To be kicked in the ribs and lose your power of speech
is to be tied to someone else's bed
of pain. To feel the snot running down your chin
is like finding yourself on a deserted beach
with nothing in your stomach or your head
but waves and pounding fists, an idiot grin.

3

You come to the place by water, and you land
on salt-sprayed concrete. Cold fury is the sea
at its most melancholic. It is the frozen hand
that shoves you ashore, scrapes at your bare knee,
and claws when you turn round. A poor estate
outside the city walls: its citizens,
working in the shipyards, congregate
to welcome you suspiciously. Their kitchens

will never see you, nor their parlours. They
take stock, hang back. They offer you advice
and sundry favours. Some of them hate you now
and go on hating you. You won't go away.
You become an object of fear. You are not as nice
as they are. You want to be but don't know how.

4

London was suburbs that seemed to stretch forever,
a vast relief map of the rich and poor
divided by bus routes, streets you crossed over,
avoiding the feet of salesmen at the door,
children who aged so fast, their blasted faces
began to sag like the plastic bags they carried,
that darkened then faded to the smelly places
they lived in, left, returned to when they married,

divorced, sickened and died. There was no
refinement in this cruelty. It was broad
and insistent, a faintly robotic hammering.
Then everything went quiet. A slow
turning away and crossing of the road.
Withdrawal, sullenness and stammering.

5

Jewboy is not this island's privilege.
That shit-hatred is common currency.
Always there are those living at the edge
of self-respect who loathe the strange, the fancy
and the vulnerable. But it's not enough.
Cold fury is what you have. You spend it
where appropriate, there's gallons of the stuff.
The hatred is universal. You never mend it.

There is a kind of silence that's specific
to a place. You enter it with respect
and make your home in it. It opens up
like a heart that is almost refusing to tick.
You become it: it is now an object
you possess and love and are afraid to drop.

6

The boys who beat up my brother are living still,
Their day is gone. They're long over the hill.
I've seen them walking down the shopping street
with carrier bags, staring at their feet.
Their shoes were scuffed, cheap trainers, heavy boots.
They wore old jeans or crumpled shiny suits.
Their hair had thinned. Their scalps were peeking through.
Their knuckles wrinkled red and white and blue.

I speak plain so they hear me. I don't think
that they will listen. I offer them a drink.
They tell me life is worse than I can guess.
They tell me, and expect some tenderness
to creep out of the language and embrace
what's left of them and the whole island race.

Solferino Violet

Once he had opened his violin-case
that inner plush overwhelmed me. I know
there is a question here, an innuendo
I don't intend to answer to your face,
like synaesthesia, or something to do
with sexuality, mother, or the bowels,
that there is a power within us which howls
at the moon. And then the old man drew
the bow across and the strings vibrated sad
and dusty answers back at me. The room
was responding to him in its turn.
This reciprocity was all we had
between us and it had begun to bloom
Judaic flowers: Oistrakh, Heifetz, Stern.

Get real, I said. These are the grandfathers
you never knew and felt no strong desire
ever to meet. Old schlocks gone to the fire
with their doilies and candles; infrequent bathers
in the Protestant sun, solemn upholders
of precedent, given to self abuse
and cancer, eternal bearers of bad news.
I was an unwilling fly on their shoulders.
I believed my own propaganda like
anyone might. I didn't want them, wished
them gone. With the floor vibrating under
my feet, I was waiting for the music to strike
some respect into me so I should feel ravished
by its omnipotent *yes* of squeal and thunder.

When thunder came I let the violet seep
into my bloodstream along with all that
ravishment. I was in a shallow sleep
where dreams move in insiduous flat
planes under the watchful eye of a mind
left unattended. And then cherries! A wood
full of cherries appeared somewhere on my blind
side, disorientating, the colour of blood.

A memory of rolling down the hill
gorged with black cherries, my mother looking on
then rolling with me. And so everything
kept rolling. I could imagine being ill
with too much sweetness, finding myself alone
with a stretch of wire, a single metal string.

Resin along horsehair. My brother stood
in front of the open window, tightening strings.
A G-Plan coffee-table, more glass than wood,
supported an ashtray and some tea things.
The suburbs were singing. He wore a quiff,
Cliff Richard style. Felix Bartholdy
waited on the stand. There was something stiff
about the day, stiff and melancholy
as the furniture. Slowly I was waking
from nightmare to a kind of lovely music.
My brother played. He really was good at it.
I accompanied him, my fingers aching
with tension and all the summer air thick
with the sound of the colour violet.

Rousing those violets, the old man ran
a couple of scales through his withered hands.
Light from the stained glass window threw bands
of colour across his fingers. He began
some other piece whose name I now forget.
I felt like leaving. I didn't want to be
wound into this, not here, in Kingsbury,
North London, staring at that violet
plush in the open case. I felt, as they say,
strangely moved. It was a long time ago.
Some thirty years. Even now the faint buzz
of the lower strings can give me away.
It's nice to think of a colour called Solferino.
Of course, I didn't then know what it was.

All In

1

At fifty I recall the *Best of British* like pork
set out on a slab. There is the ringside and there
is our friend, Tibor, the wrestler. It is hot work
being thrown about. My father and I stare
horrified at his violent transformation
into gristle. Bruise after bruise appears.
We feel indecent in the foreign commotion.
My father shakes. I'm on the edge of tears.
This is the empire, the gladiatorial
climax of something tough and full of spit.
We don't recognise it as such, but a vast
weight is collapsing in the inquisitorial
balance. We can't bear to look at it.
When the lights come up we disappear fast.

2

We disappear fast, much as we always do
at times like this. A sexual drone begins
as on a distant bagpipe. Someone is falling through
the ropes. A woman adjusts her dress. Light thins
to dust. Bodies move as if in a mirror.
There's too much flesh in the world, too much blood
in the veins. Beckmann. Balthus. Burra.
Heavy thighs push through a field of mud.
There is a language for this and I am trying
to speak it. It is an old clock that shudders
in the corner of a boarding house: *glug*, *glug*
it says. On the window-ledge flies are dying
on their backs. Inside it, cloud shadows
billow across the bathroom shaving mug.

3

Big Daddy is about to splash from ropes.
His enormous belly sways as he climbs up
straddling the post. The other man gropes
the air like a crocked spider, waits for him to flop.
The sadness in their eyes crawls out with them,
emerging from headlocks, nelsons, shoulderpins.
Their strangleholds delicate as the stem
of a wine glass when the big party begins.
They are nobility in the abstract, bodies beautiful
cradling wounded minds. Their lovers touch
their hidden softness with solicitude,
turning them into butterflies, light bulls
in lost china shops. Nothing is too much
for them to ask, no single touch too crude.

4

My father and I recoil from violence.
He hits me once and there's an end of that.
I don't hit back. We're living in a tense
empire that could fall and squash us flat.
It's slowly falling now but there is time
to roll away in one well practised ruse.
The map beneath us shifts and burns like lime,
its scarlet territories are a bruise
that will not heal too fast. But here we are
and here is Tibor flying through the air,
a human projectile about to crash.
The sport is low, but he's a shooting star.
He hits the ground, he brushes back his hair
and waits to loose his trademark forearm smash.

The Umbrellas

Even now I cannot help thinking of them
as historical. The noise they make drowns
out the radio static of the street. Grey gowns
of rain flutter or run away in a million gem
spectacular but these dark suns expand
and guard us from the present danger which
is simply a drench of brilliants, rich
as the flood. Look, children, I hold out my hand
beyond its perimeter fence. The fine
spray gathers in my palm then dies away.
I close the black sun and hobble off with it.
It sighs as it closes, approximates to a line
or a stick, like the day before yesterday,
or the meetings of a wartime cabinet.

White Hart Lane

(for Francis Gilbert)

It hardly matters now. But it was there:
the stadium with its single focus, and you,
fragmented, anxious, someone they let through
with gestures of diffused paternal care

because you too were to be initiated
into what they were, which made you proud,
yet careful. You were and were not the crowd,
its passions high, ironic, understated,

brutal, like an earthquake just beginning
with a drumming of feet and the small roar
rising as teams appeared on the far side

dappling the pitch. You watched the notion of winning
and losing harden into focus and kept score
of everything, the small matter of pride.

*

It's premonition. The whole thing's premonition
and there's the poetry. The lilac team
is (phonetic) Dózha. Do you remem-
ber? Time is fracture and compression,

like this line. They're only names you recall
with a certain vividness. But later
when the ball came your way, like rainwater
in a winter pantomime, like any ball

a challenge, a threat, something personal
and you practised juggling with it or ran
zigzags between markers, you were chosen.

The hours you spent by a suburban brick wall
in northwest London! You were already a man
without a future, as if all time had frozen.

*

It is what dance is, only with a brief
dumb purpose: courage, grace, power, speed and guile
at the service of pride glimpsed through a turnstile,
accompanied by the sharp, interim grief

of any loss. Even a dull game will serve
to keep things ticking over and the great ones
survive in fragments beyond their seasons
in a leap, or run, or tackle, or body-swerve...

But I'm dumb, like everyone else. It is the way
it must be, that you must understand:
it's what we are, who can't speak or dare to think

that it or we matter. It's just another day
in the league. I hold my father's hand
both of us pitched forward, on the terrace brink.

Spring Green

Three apocalyptic grotesques

Think of it at the feet of a young dandy
in emblematic Tudor costume: part
nature, part intellect, much like the heart
he wears on his full sleeve. Romantic, randy

and common as grass painted by a child
in her first school; look, it runs down the page
and dribbles onto the desk, an image
of everything that is innocuous and wild...

White rabbits, mushrooms, snails, blackberrying,
the sherbet dip with liquorice stick, pence
in purses. He is dreaming of her hand

white as a sugar mouse, of burying
his head in her breasts in a green nonsense
of lawns and roses, somewhere in England.

*

The floral clock moves round from light to shade.
The boarding houses rattle with visitors.
It is *Brighton Rock*, Sid James, Diana Dors,
Brylcreem and Phyllosan and Lucozade.

Dirk Bogarde kills Jack Warner. The Duke of Squat
dances with Miss Fiona FitzFollicle
at her coming out party. A spherical
moon is lightly balanced on the scout hut.

The grass in *Genevieve* glimmers like yards
of cloth in a tailor's shop. Kenneth More
perspires gently in the August sun.

Along the sea-front men are buying postcards
of the promenade. West Indies score
freely on a green wicket. Time moves on.

*

A perfect greenness, everything is neat.
I'm back in the springtime of a realm
of primary colours which overwhelm
desire, back at the young dandy's feet

among earthworms, beetles, between the blades
of individual grass from which depend
bright beads of dew. It is, I think, the end
of the world. Birds are singing serenades

to the great chain of being for the last
time. Someone is slicing up a cow.
Someone bottles the spaces between things.

Life is kissing and telling, but telling it fast
as if there were always and only a single now,
a spring to cap and end all other springs.

The Ropes

There was a hut a mile along the cliff
where cub scouts gathered. Here they learnt the ropes
and how to tie them into useful shapes.
It was a chapter in their faux-naif
childhood, since time was passing and quite soon
there would be no more children. The adult
winds, the massive grown-up sea, the old salt
in the mature parlour; late afternoon
for a Phyllosan culture in climacteric
decline. The ropes were only the words
anyone used, sagging a little, loose
as old clothes and the ancient air was thick
and hoarse, the cliff crowded with blue birds,
sheepshanks and reef-knots tightening to a noose.

Payne's Grey

The sea at night off Dover. Waves gloss rock,
move mirrorwise into profounder darkness
reflecting nothing. Time is a wind-up clock
in a lost pocket of its formal dress.
It slips in minor flashes off the crest
of all that's visible and proceeds to swim
away to where whole centuries are pressed
to fossil. Even the thought of them is dim,
and this polite, most English of grey tones
settles across them like a woollen shroud,
casts shadows between the finest of fine bones,
finds tired faces in a homebound crowd
of football supporters at half past five who feel
the grey sea at their backs like naked steel.

Sepia: The Light Brigade

A late spring rain has washed the field away.
Skin shows beneath the skin. A pallid smudge
of earth turns into marsh, to a dead language.
Under the grass long smears of human clay
lie down and rise, lie down again, and walk
into low cloud as if into lines of fire.
A couple on the path. A woman. An entire
family out for a stroll. The leaves talk

in ghost whispers and a bird reiterates
its single warning that life attends on fear,
that every green must turn to sepia.
The future looks on patiently and waits
clipping its fingernails, tugging at its ear.
The landscape yawns, grows steadily sleepier.

Copper Brown

And when it was worn smooth, a Victorian bun
with all its features drowned, obliterate,
a kind of pessary or wafer, without date
or motto, when it could hardly hurt anyone,
under a garden clod or in a forgotten tin
along with buttons, old stamps, bits of lace,
with its horrendous apology for a face,
a half-cock ghost next to a rusty pin,
it still disturbed, if only for the hands
you knew had touched it once, its princely sum
part of a historical continuum
that would eventually present its strict demands,
when it would stand there pounding at your door
like death in the simple annals of the poor.

In the Greek Restaurant

Sometimes I dream I am swimming. Afternoon.
The sun shines in the window across the bed
which still has not been made, curiously slanted.
And from downstairs comes the sound of a cartoon
with jerky music. My tail goes *twitch, twitch, twitch*.
I am a big fish in a small pond. And then I wake.
It's time to start cooking, get the plates out, make
the tables ready, prepare another rich
but neutered stew. The kitchen grows quite hot.
We swig a little wine, keep working till six
then relax a little. Great big gouts of steam
hang by the ceiling over the open pot.
A distant radio plays. The wall-clock ticks
inside my head, the kettle emits a dying scream...

To have come so far and then to find the street
reasonable but no more, the weather dull
with not much passing trade when pubs are full,
a market nearby, occasionally to meet
old friends who might help out, the children set
for business or professions at some school
and your hair thinning, your eyes like cat's drool,
saying hello to the old girl with the hairnet...
It isn't good enough. But then your countrymen
drag their ghosts in, pour out a few drinks...
a bit of *folklor* for the visitors...
the odd loud fight or quarrel now and then...
and deep in the night the darkly spreading inks
of squids across vast glimmering kitchen floors.

Coolidge in Indigo

There are bad scenes. The film with the jagged
edge between two murders when the curtain
moves and the child stands lost and uncertain
staring at shadows, imagining the haggard
face of his mother opening her mouth wide
and the sound of a fly, the simmering
of a pan and the distant clock glimmering
like his image in the window, multiplied
as if for ever between two moments. So
into that dusk came Coolidge, its shuttered
general store and desolate garage
trailing off into dust which seemed to blow
from nameless places where nothing had mattered
for years or suffered some terminal haemorrhage.

Then Anthony got out to check the map.
Three or four men glanced over. They were poor,
the kind who lend themselves to metaphor
with nothing else to lend, caught in a trap
which had closed over them. Their mouths closed
over each other in that twilight, stranger
than cinema. Each one smelled of danger,
of damp but flammable rooms. They posed
in their dreamscape like symbols, long detached
from anywhere but the desert and the long
featureless road where station-wagons rusted.
This was a bad moment. My foot gently touched
the gas pedal. Something was wrong
with the map in which we had naively trusted.

And then the road trailed off and hot dust threw
itself against the tight window. A road sign
pointed to towns way off the marked line.
The thin Arizona wind gathered and blew
vague traffic past us, and later we arrived
in some lit town, and later still in Scottsdale,
in time for our dinner date. The night was stale
with relief. We felt we had survived
some insignificance. Our host waited

in the lobby and we drove off to a vast
inedible dinner. The sky was indigo,
with many stars like something inflated.
Our host was counting his credit cards. At last
he found his preferred option and we could go.

Kayenta Black

Some time through dinner Freddie Ganado said
he'd worn black for six years but recently
gave all that up. His clothes looked black to me,
but no, he said, they were dark blue. We had
arrived in Flagstaff, having left behind
the reservation with its thick despairs.
Kayenta, torrential rain. Rows of school chairs.
One attractive girl had made up her mind
to be the first Navajo US president.
Sharp as hell but suicidal, our host
informed us as she drove us down the road
to Monument Valley, herself a monument.
After seventeen years she resigned her post
from sheer frustration. And so the story flowed

as we flew on. And she had organised
a ropes project, a kind of confidence
or bonding exercise, and this made sense
right here where Indian stores advertised
trinkets and rugs next to a row of shacks.
We took pictures and read poems to a few
more students that evening while a cold wind blew
fresh and hard outside down quiet dirt tracks.
One shy and silent boy offered us discreet
gifts of turquoise. We thanked each other
effusively. He left. We talked and wrote
down names. It was sacramental and sweet,
like taking leave of a daughter or a mother,
a gentle, heartfelt clearing of the throat.

Freddie said he wanted a synthesis
between Kerouac and the Navajo religion,
it was something he could clearly imagine.
Indeed he was desperate to achieve this.
His girlfriend had chucked him. He was very young.
After the reading we all drove into town
and bought him a bottle of pale Newcastle Brown
he could not finish because it was too strong.
Sadness oozed from him, and hope. His face was

very beautiful but life was hard. Meanwhile
the leader of the pipe band was engaged
in conversation with Ian and the buzz
of the bar grew louder and Freddie gave a smile
so tired and lost it seemed the world had aged.

And I thought back to the dinner party where
Pedro's wife – a Berkeley graduate –
spoke haltingly above her untouched plate
of *vol-au-vents*. She too was in despair
and lost in this impromptu gathering.
She said it was a civilised neighbourhood
then they both left. The food was very good,
our hostess kind, and there was Freddie sitting
in black which he said was blue. Round my neck
the turquoise stone I had been given by
the silent boy in Kayenta, silent as a mouse
but six foot high and sixteen stone, in black.
So I talked on amused and flattered by
the crisp intelligent daughters of the house.

Azure

Barney Kessel strums at the smoky air
then in comes Ella. The breath she expels
has something steely about it. It smells
of perfume and aggressive hardware.

Outside: cars and the waiting universe
that catches onto warmth and chills it through,
while further up, the stars are full of blue
distances gathering to rehearse.

Somewhere beyond numbers the word *soul*
drifts with its meteor showers and dead suns,
detached from meaning like a piece of trash...

Dreaming, drifting, sings Ella, in control.
But out among the tables soul outruns
body and slowly burns down to fine ash.

*

Meanwhile a girl is flagging down a taxi,
a couple look through a window, and upstairs,
alone in the world of tables and chairs,
a small boy tunes in to the galaxy,

his fingers scrabbling on the keyboard. His eyes
don't need to look down. The world unwraps
itself behind the screen as he thinks and taps
out messages. Next door a baby cries,

someone is watching TV or a video.
Ella is on the record, singing this.
His sisters plays, parents get on with things.

Even the universe needs somewhere to go
so why not here? Later, the parents kiss
their children. *Drifting... dreaming... azure...* Ella sings.

*

Later, much later. Not Ella but Parker and Dizzy
throwing in White Christmas for Bud Powell,
and as the doomed boppers disembowel
another tune and the waitresses are busy

with the drunks on Thirteen, the boy revises
his A level maths and plays a little music
waiting for it to settle in. Bird's lick
follows some hidden line, loops and rises,

ties things together in a loose kind of way.
The soul inspects itself in a buckled mirror,
notices its eyes and its set of lip,

forgives its nose, appears a touch *distrait*
by its own standards, feels a vague terror
at any suggestion it might lose its grip.

*

Then Miles and cool. The lost soul turns its back
on the audience and blows to itself. That low
piercing dull indifferent cry moves below
the ocean surface among bladderwrack

and silence. Elsewhere dead rocks wheel
about a dying planet. The eye itself rolls
like a stone. Miles stands stiffly or strolls
about the stage like the whole gig wasn't real

but happened in his head. And the boy is reading
another text book, and the waitress serves
another table with another drunk,

and the evening goes on gently bleeding
into dawn. Suddenly the music swerves
into dance mode, the harsh jag-jag of funk.

*

Funk with the Brecker Brothers. A rapper from
Tottenham Hale in a converted garage.
Jungle's rapid displacements haemorrhage
at three-thirty a.m. under the eardrum.

A tiny luminous figure flits across the screen
collecting prizes, upping the body count.
An elder watches as the high scores mount.
Way off the pace, he's scanning a magazine

that advertises technical wizardry.
Sound, speed, adrenalin: soul food. Outside
rain is quietly cooling itself in the gutter.

It's what we have, our last ditch decency,
a cool hand across the street, the long slide
of water on glass, the fingers' chronic stutter.

*

Azure, sings Ella, undisturbed by this,
being herself another recording lost
in her own listening. Static settles like frost
on Fats Waller. A kind of paralysis

blights Joplin, and Frank O'Hara is as dead
as Billie Holliday. All sink in the night.
There's no such thing as satisfied appetite
in the living museum. The boy's head

contains his soul as it runs down his arms,
through his fingers, into a pool of distance.
Desire is the stars for which there is no cure,

metallic, silvery perhaps, moving in swarms
across darkness without any resistance
inimitable, dislocated, pure.

Figures at the Baths

1

Those figures emerging from the water are men
of an indeterminate period and age.
Their hair had long ago begun to flatten
against their scalps. They became pure image
almost as soon as they entered, and rising,
were transformed into a kind of secret.
The world is old to them. There is nothing surprising
left in it. Even the bottomless water is set
into a basin of marble which has always
been there. Classical columns wear the light
with a knowing patience. They know nothing of days
or hours, of wind or weather, or morning or night,
but know where they've been and know the deep
undrowned existence anticipating sleep.

2

Norfolk in January. Rain, icy cold, goes on
and off all day. The wind is like barbed wire
and the sun brings no relief. There is someone
running down the road, his hair and coat on fire.
The birthing pool, the baths, the classical
columns are consolations of memory.
You see their glowing surfaces with their trickle
of light. You hear the men move. Their furry
bodies are sleek with cold. Our eyes touch
across the room. They flare at the point of contact
as if one of us had suddenly lit a match,
as if meaning had shrunk to this single act,
as if time had begun to slip but hung there
at the edge of the pool flattening our hair.

Dog-Latin

The thing that I was was changing. Or was
it wishful thinking? The train rolled on
through a shower, spraying itself in million-
fractured glass and I was lost in the fuzz
of voices – mobile phones, newspapers, leaves
in a long wind. Houses drifted by, caught
in the rain-net, held together by taut
wires: blood, loss, distant relatives
talking in their sleep. Here day and night
made little difference. A man reading the *Mail*
adjusted his glasses. Another had put down
an empty burger-box which opened its bright
yellow mouth and breathed a pungent trail
of garnish across the fast retreating town.

Disjecta membra, little splinters of dog-
Latin from schooldays, as if all life was this,
asserting its privileges, wanting a last kiss
before the terminal parting into fog
and more rain. I looked at the ends of my fingers
parked on the table before me. The train
shook them slightly as it might shake a chain
of events. Everywhere, passengers
were becoming residents, workers, emissaries.
Something was crumbling – a people possibly,
and the flags in the garage had set up
a mad flutter under the bending trees.
It was night or morning or midday, and we
were sitting still, waiting for it to stop.

Golden Boy

Once I was the golden boy, beloved:
a woman laid me down inside a pram,
but who can tell me now whose child I am?
The years go by and who knows what I've suffered?
She brought me things once, tickled me and kissed
my plump pink cheeks. Believe me, when I cried
she came running with comforts, mortified.
Who thinks in childhood, I will not be missed?
Who thinks, *My golden age will pass away
and turn to lead?* That knowledge creeps on slow
but unexpected, when you're lying in a doorway
vaguely aware of feet that come and go.
But I was golden then and slept so long
no one was left to tell me where I belong.

The golden boy for ever on the run,
whether he runs with beasts or runs alone,
finds cold is singular, within the bone.
I look back and I can't tell what I've done
in all these years or when I turned to gold,
whether the toes came first, or fingertips
and when the transformation reached my lips,
when my poor guts were colonised by cold
which ate into my marrow with its teeth.
All I know's the heart that keeps on ticking,
its metric beat persistent underneath
the ribs that time is gradually unpicking.
I see myself in gold which might be lead,
but no one knows that down among the dead.

War Is Over

(for Anthony Thwaite)

One of those wet Junes with the skylight tapping
its fingernails on the thin drum of the house.

Yesterday, in the underground, a dark brown mouse
ran zigzag between live rails, vaguely unwrapping
the present of its small life, and when the train came,
the mouse disappeared beneath it. Along from us
a woman was writing a letter with ferocious
concentration, her lips constantly moving to frame
the words as the letters appeared. Beside her
an Asian girl was reading Jane Austen, a boy
dived for an empty seat. The war was over,
said someone's paper. There was little joy
on the faces, it was much as usual. Permanent night
down here. Upstairs, the emergence into daylight.

Visitations

As one comes in another goes out. As one
shakes out a tablecloth another is eating
a hearty meal. As one sits down alone
another listens to his lover's heart beating.

As one prays for deliverance, another
delivers a letter or an explosive device.
As one gathers the harvest, his brother
lies in the doorway. As one finds a nice

coincidence between numbers, his neighbour
sees his coins disappear down the waiting slot.
As one man examines the fruit of his labour
his shadow tells beads, counts peas into the pot

or stars in the sky and feels the night wind blowing
on his face with all this coming and going.

*

As one goes out, the other comes in. It is light
in the window where the angel bends
over the stove giving the virgin a fright.
It is bright at the top of the house where the road ends.

There's a distinct touch of gold in the gutter
running with beer. There is translucence
in the chipped saucer with its rim of used butter.
There's a glow on TV. There's a faint sense

of the luminous numinous in the alarm clock
set for six in the morning and a kind of shine
in the mirror the angels have learned to unlock
and enter suddenly and an even harder to define

radiance in the skin, in the shock of dawn
with sheet turned down and bedroom curtains drawn.

Cromer Green at the Regency Café

I used to wonder at the old ones sitting
in cars parked neatly opposite the sea
with Sunday papers in their laps, steadily
dozing near uneventful water, knitting
in silence, reading, waiting. What was the sense
of congregating here with weathered faces
beside these terminal railings in places
that signalled departure and indifference?
The sadness of the English, I thought. Odd
how they folded in on themselves at last,
something serious must have happened here
under the jurisdiction of this grey-green god
they weren't exactly worshipping, but cast
respectful glances at across the pier.

Out on the pier a three-legged dog beamed
happily at its master. Water fribbled and scrabbled
below the walkway, laughing at some ribald
double-entendre. Someone must have dreamed
all this at a time of comic anxiety.
Fisherman were casting their last lines.
Great towering hotels flashed gleeful signs.
The moon rose over the building society.
Boys were trying to surf into the stones
along the beach. Someone had thrown away
a *Daily Mail* which was carried by a gust
past cartons and upended ice-cream cones.
There were cups of tea at the Regency Café
and cod and chips on tables covered in dust.

There was nothing to say about this. It was
saying itself in the language of self-delight,
beautiful and formed, talking in spite
of us through its own generated grammars
in a kind of English no one actually spoke,
leaving behind a faint linguistic trace
like a historical essence, a lost grace
that no one act of history could revoke.
Now the wind was rising. Waves were barred

with patches of pure colour, each a shimmer
in the coming dusk with echoes of dying sound,
but clearly defined, the image sharp and hard.
A brilliant half rainbow was growing dimmer,
retreating to its source beneath the ground.

I could imagine being one of the old,
staying here for ever, staring past
the lit pier and searching the overcast
sky for the moon in the growing cold.
Nature was peopled with coherent signs
that anyone could read. The waitress brought
the bill and we stood up. It was a short
journey home and we should start it... Lines
of lightbulbs were gently swaying outside
and the wind was fresh from the north. Our car
waited, parked with all the rest in the drive
by the sunken gardens. Another seagull cried
below us. Lights were glowing in the bar
of The Ship and the old were still alive.

Great Yarmouth

The sea was black and far beyond the sand
an icy gust blew between whatever shelter
the promenade offered. Life was out of kilter
in the world and here was proof. A bright band

of amusement arcades caught the full force
of the wind. Their hyperactivity
was manic, all lights flashing, each a city
in its final throes. A tiny fairground horse

whinnied at *The House of the Dead* where ghouls
materialised and were cut down in a spray
of music. The place was empty but men lay
on stone steps, buckled and broken in pools

of flat Sega blood, and everywhere the roar
of tiny coins and pebbles on the shore.

*

Out of kilter and broken. Late winter light,
which is to say, no light at all, except this.
And it was buzzing and flashing, its synapses
wholly preoccupied, breath short, chest tight,

sweating slightly. Rank upon brilliant rank
of potential cardiac arrest, and all for nothing.
It was the latest gothic passing its dark wing
over the empty seafront on its way to the blood bank.

And here was England, shouting at the sea,
a single bent figure glaring behind the change desk,
surveying its domain, the new grotesque.
It was terrible to see it. Outside the fresh, free

silence and the barren wind, a fast car,
the darkness vast, without a single star.

Punctuation

It was a matter of language. The glottal swell
of waves as its long tongue came pitching in
lapping at land. Words were shedding their skin
on the beach to leave behind the dying smell

of creosote. It was all sadness there.
I watched amused as rain-swollen clouds swam
across the sky from nearby Sheringham
dropping a few fat drops in the thick air.

The light brimmed over somewhere at the edge,
a double rainbow sprang from a beached boat
and stopped abruptly in a wedge of dark.

There were a few cars parked along the ledge
and close to shore a bobbing bright red float
like some arbitrary punctuation mark.

Backwaters: Norfolk Fields
(for W.G. Sebald)

1

Backwaters. Long grass. Slow speech. Far off
a truck heaves its load of rust into a yard
next to a warehouse full of office furniture
no one will ever use, unless to stuff
some temporary room when times are hard.
Across the fields the sweet smell of manure.

We're years behind. Even our vowels sag
in the cold wind. We have our beauty spots
that people visit and leave alone, down main
arterials and side roads. A paper bag
floats along the beach. Clouds drift in clots
of grey and eventually down comes the rain.

We're at the end. It might simply be of weather
or empire or of something else altogether.

2

Empire perhaps. Chapels in the cathedral.
Old airstrips. History's human noises
still revving down a field. Clothes pegs hang
like hanged men. It is all procedural.
Resentment simmers in the empty houses.
The wind at its eternal droning harangue.

I'm wanting to mouth the word that fits the case
but it's like trying to roll a shadow from
the street where it has been sitting for years.
It will not go. You cannot wipe the face
of the clock or restore a vanished kingdom.
You feel the shape of the thing between your ears.

Your mouth is talking to the steady light
which listens to you and remains polite.

3

How beautiful the place is. Watch it hold
time still. I want you to tell me what this is,
this place at the back of beyond, in the sun
that retains its distance in a pale gold
mirror, minding its own brilliant business,
not in the habit of speaking to anyone.

Here is a man who loves cars. He has bought
a house on something very like a hill.
He fills his yard up with old cars. He mends things –
roofs, walls. He's biblical. He does not take thought
for the morrow, won't worry when he falls ill.
He goes swooping along on welded wings,

his children unruly, his wife losing heart.
The beautiful is what keeps them apart.

4

The WI stall. Jams, flowers. White
hair scraped back in the draught of an open door.
The butcher's. He knows you by name. He calls
your name out. His chopping block is washed bright
by the morning sun. The solicitor
down the street. His nameplate. War memorials

with more names. Rows of Standleys, Bunns,
Myhills, Kerridges. Names on shopfronts: bold
reds, whites and blues in stock typography.
Names on labels tied with string to shotguns.
Names on electoral registers. Names in gold
in the children's section of the cemetery

by the railway cuttings. Willows, faint blue
in the afternoon, light gently whistles through.

5

Too easy all this, like a fatal charm
intended to lull you into acquiescence.
Think karaoke. Sky. The video shop.
Broken windows. The sheer boredom. The alarm
wailing at two am. The police presence.
Pastoral graffiti on the bus stop.

Think back of the back of beyond "beyond". End
of a line. The sheer ravishing beauty
of it as it runs into the cold swell
of the North Sea, impossible to comprehend.
The harsh home truisms of geometry
that flatten to a simple parallel.

This is your otherness where the exotic
appears by a kind of homely conjuring trick.

6

A 1580s mural. A hunting scene
runs right around the room. A trace of Rubens,
Jordaens, a touch, even, of Chinese
in the calligraphic lines. Experts clean
the powdery limewash, two PhD students
from the university, anxious to please.

A strange dome appears, out of period
somewhere near the top. Even here
there's something far flung in the code
of a different language, another God
extolling other virtues, a pioneer
morality just waiting to explode.

Flemish brickwork. Devastation. Riders
exploring hidden walls with snails and spiders.

7

You're out at the end of the pier. It is winter.
Tall waves splutter underfoot. Gulls pirouette
and dive into dark grey. The radio is alive
with music. Its tiny voices seem to splinter
into sharp distinct consonants. You forget
the time of day. It's someone else's narrative

buzzing beneath you. New explorers come
out of the light to exploit the heart of darkness.
The world is inside out, exposed as never before.
Water and sky are a continuum.
A terrible gaiety rustles the sea like a dress
it must discard. It sweeps by just once more

then drops across the beach and remains there
in the memory, in ghosted, mangled air.

8

How beautiful it is, this silence waiting
on salt. The disused railway lines between
wild blackberries. The faint hum of stray flies
on windowsills. Time is accelerating
down the coast road leaving behind a clean
pair of heels and a whiff of paradise.

The man with welded wings roars past, in love
with reason. His wife leaves in a freak gust,
their children flying along. Dogs race across
the walls in search of a lost treasure trove.
Gently idling, vast trucks deposit rust
in empty yards with patches of dry grass.

Broad fields out of town. The slow unravelling
of a long reel where everyone is travelling.

9

Travelling through or ending. The damp house
beyond the library where an old woman
has been retreating for some fifty years,
and still retreats towards a dangerous
blind alley, towards a corner, where the nearest demon
might swallow her up leaving no more tears.

There are none left to shed in the overgrown
garden with its coarse weeds. It is as if
she had been sleeping a century or more,
without a retinue, simply on her own,
growing ever more querulous, ever more stiff
till rigor mortis had frozen her four score

into zero. Country aristocracy.
The dead fields at their last-gasp fantasy.

10

A place full of old women. Hardy, courageous,
muttering to themselves and others in cafés,
engaging unwilling partners in conversation,
accosting young men, making outrageous
advances to middle-aged couples with tea-trays,
embarassing husbands with their ostentation.

Old men in betting shops peering to check
the odds. Old men, natty in white, creaking
over bowls, with Beryl Cook elegance.
Old men tottering, sticking out a neck
at the neighbour while the latter is speaking.
Old men in the church hall learning to dance.

The old in their gerontopolis. At home
in sheltered housing, under the pleasure dome.

11

How many times do I have to say the word: End!
and still not end. You can't go further than
the sea, not on a motorway. And what
are you doing here, yes, you and your friend
from Morocco, Uganda, St Kitts or Pakistan?
Whatever has brought you to this far, flat

kingdom with its glum farmers? Surely you
don't think this is America where dreams
are the given, where you swear allegiance
to a new self? Have you somehow fallen through
the net of the world to be lost among reams
of legislature in these alien regions?

Homing. We are homing to the sea. Back
where we never were, at the end of the track.

12

On a high-cloud day, you could drown in sky
round here. You see the gentle swaying
of leaves along a wall. Something under
the water, under the skylight, in the dry
cabin under the ocean is quietly playing
a music of muted bells in soft thunder.

It is eating you away until you've gone,
like the spider scurrying up its own spit
back to its natural centre in the dark,
and the sky remains enormous. Someone
is watching the house-martin, the blue tit,
the tiny insects making their tiny mark

in the grass, and the small rain that falls far
across the field as on a distant star.

Haydn

1

No wind at all. The clothes-pegs on the line
are hardly shivering. An even grey
has closed the world off. It is Saturday
in the quiet towns of the east. A fine
distinction between two adjacent tones
of sea and air carries no distant cries
or the light dust of ground or broken bones.
There are no fresh news in the mouths of flies.

No flies at all. No wasps. No bees. Nothing come
nor gone. The day stands like an untouched drum:
Haydn on Radio Three. Letters in the tray.
It is the spaces in between that are dissembling.
The neighbours are asleep or gone away.
Nothing now can set the clothes-pegs trembling.

2

One syllable short. How does anything get in
to this stoppered corner of England where
the dust is the dust of the fields, layer on layer,
and the grass is a tight comfortable skin
in the churchyard by a ruined monastery?
The lost incomprehensible syllable is stuck
in the throat: the bones' dying industry
winds down like an old tenement block.

Until it blows. Until the fuse catches the thumb
that triggers it in the distant capital or the screen
by the wall and the fields are suddenly dumb.
Until a faint red seeps beneath the green
among ground elder, earthworms, and the lost
coins of the realm bent and scaled with rust.

Gone Fishing

Jack, assistant shopman, retired from the force,
makes fishing-rods. His Polish father's dead,
(ex-wartime flier). Jack reserves his hatred
for Uncle Joe of Russia, but, in due course

follow murderers, burglars, gypsies, queers,
Pakis, paedophiles... Oh, the lies we're told!...
he grows angry. The long-lost foreign old
are turning in their graves, giving faint cheers

for anglers by gravel pits, for the cold North Sea
lumbered with dark and fish, for winds from the pole
that blow the socks off us, cheers for summer, our sole
delight that appears, brightly, suddenly,

its pitiless eye fixed on the very spot
we're standing on. And will be, like as not.

Flash

When she looked through the view-finder she found
him changed. It was the shadow of a moment
that made the difference, one in a vast torrent
of light that seemed to have lifted her from the ground.
Perhaps the bomb had finally fallen. He
was still smiling but had dropped through a trapdoor
on the other side of the world. No more
time was left, it was all eternity.

Then she pressed the shutter and it went click
as it always does, and there he was, smiling
but elsewhere. Elsewhere was where they both were.
And it was green, attractive, beguiling
as they returned, the earth steady and pure,
washed clean, as if by hypo or by magic.

Viridian

I woke to viridian. Across the square
the rain was falling in a fleece of light
and clouds were endless. A girl with dripping hair
was hurrying across, her coat pulled tight
about her. A pair of wagtails twitched and rose
from the grass which was gradually darkening
to one deep bass note at which music froze.
Only fat raindrops were prepared to sing.

Against this the thin brightness of laughter set
itself. There it was. Someone was laughing below,
on another floor, as if all that was lost
had been briefly recovered, never to be let
go of. Her laugh was against the letting go
despite the rain that settled thick as dust.

AN ENGLISH APOCALYPSE
(for Dennis O'Driscoll)

Gladdith anon, thou lusty Troy Novaunt,
Citie that some tyme cleped was New Troy

WILLIAM DUNBAR

Prologue: The Fire Film

It was the day the cows came down in dollops
of thick snow. Sheep followed as sheep will
landing head first, their legs like lollipops

or dead matches that still fired. Every hill
on the coastline was burning. It was Bonfire Night.
I watched the children run among dead cattle

clutching sparklers, gaping at rockets in full flight
from the plastic tubes that housed them. We were going
up in smoke, but gaily. It would be all right

to run riot now, to feel blood flowing
in our narrow veins and think of carnival.
Our faces were fire-lit masks. We were growing

into our archetypes, part-human, part-animal.
One wore a calf's head, another pranced on goat feet.
We were as we had been before our own arrival

in the fig leaf of custodianship. The High Street
was blazing more brilliantly than it had last Christmas
and the wind whistled above us, dark and sweet,

from a film set in Africa or maybe somewhere else.

1 PASTORALS
(for Katie Donovan)

Jerusalem

The leaves are nodding. The traffic runs on.
It is like opening a door on a great secret,
or drawing a dusty 1950s curtain,

a passport to a country of eternal regret,
the Old Jerusalem, a forsaken garden
where the sun is always about to set

on an empire laying down its burden.
Which is what pastoral means: life in a field
of death, natural activity as boredom,

the air crowded with unreconciled
facts: dust, light, insects, birds, sheer noise,
the plants' upward drive, their fates sealed

while they blossom with disturbing poise
that reeks of drama, waving red hands
in the air with showbiz gestures, like boys

in the band, or settle in brilliant islands
of loose coral, because summer is exotic
in such country and makes peculiar demands

on the attention, but the air is thick
with the noise of the past, so it is hard to see
what it is made of, what all this rhetoric

is actually about. Something is ominously
gathering in the sky. The clouds rise
and darken like shadows under a bright tree.

Anxiety

A man and woman at a dinner party. Their eyes
entirely elsewhere. Money problems. Below:
the park, the Thames, the hopeful strategies

of mere survival, going with the flow.
Her face reddens. Little wrinkles crowd
about her mouth, having nowhere else to go.

She has the look of the wounded and once proud.
It is heartbreaking and edgy. The tiny room
is all synapses and electricity, loud

with unspoken fear. The sky is a faint plume
of smoke over London, beyond the window glass;
clouds skate along on rims of polished chrome.

Something glints in the trees and the grass,
a thin blade of water, and the first rain
sliding down the slope of the underpass.

Fragile chains dangle from the sky. There is a stain
on the carpet but it could be shadow. Tiny wires
wrap the street in silver, folding towards the drain

from long trails of stationary tyres.
She wipes her eye, looks down at her fork,
and makes as much noise as table talk requires.

The Ark

It is night in the zoo of the universe. Stars lurk
behind soft mountains and the moon dips
under water. The dreams are getting to work.

He hooks his fingers into her waistband. She slips
towards him and raises her left knee to cover
his right thigh. Her finger rests on his lips,

then moves down to his neck. He rolls her over
and traces her spine with his chin. Her head
is turned on its side as she feels him hover

above her. Her right arm is off the bed,
touching the floor. Night giggles up its sleeve.
His teeth close as if on fresh baked bread.

And then she mounts him. They begin to heave
against the tide. They are ploughing through
the waves of the sheets, steady, purposive

voyagers. Out in the field a distraught ewe
calls to her lambs. An owl hoots in the mist.
It is stormy. They are the ship's crew.

Now he's on top, his fingers round her wrist.
She strains to kiss them. The cat in the car park
leaps from bonnet to bonnet. They want to twist

round so he's behind. It takes a sudden jerk –
and there they are. Her breasts hang below her
like any creature's, in the enormous ark

they both occupy. The beasts are beginning to stir
in the hold. She plays him like a piper.
The world is pain and stars in a cradle of fur.

The rainforests of Brazil are made of tissue-paper
that rustles in her head. He is whale blubber
in the Atlantic, a well fed grouper.

Victoriana

Pastoral is a voice in the shrubbery,
the sound of a tennis ball, a lawn where croquet
is being played by flamingoes with rubbery

elegance, the arrival of a bouquet
in a cellophane wrapper. It is mud
on the boots, a hint of dung on the parquet

of the dining room. It is the English God
at his prayers in a Victorian chapel,
the compulsive criminal up before *me lud*.

It is a kind of loss. The street is full of people
going about their shopping. The newsagent-
cum-post office. The buses. The municipal

authority's proceedings. The war monument.
It is Giovanni's cafe and Faroukh's *couscous*
in the region's only Moroccan restaurant.

It is this *res publicum* of loose
alliances. The Australian botanist
meeting the lecturer from Belarus

in a garden of old roses. The narrow wrist
encircled by a man's fingers. The rough
chest his lover has delicately kissed

while sheep bleat through the night. It is the stuff
that dreams are made of, the years and hours
of which none of them could ever have enough.

Survivor

You wake. It's as if time had bound your feet
to keep them delicate. Everything seems the same,
teetering on its lightness. There is a sweet

smear of sunlight narrowing to a flame
on the wall beside the bed. How old you are
is a secret. Nobody knows your name.

You are together in a spectacular
success that no one recognises. The news,
the *Today* programme, pass in a blur.

You have survived the millennium, are free to choose
from clothes in the wardrobe. You get dressed.
You comb your hair, brush teeth, put on your shoes.

The day is waiting. It gently cups your breast
and kisses your lips. You're away in your own
version of pastoral which is compressed

into such moments. The pair of you have grown
alabaster wings. You embrace like sculpture.
You whisper the word 'love'. It is the unknown.

It is, and always has been, the only possible future.

(for Gerald Dawe)

Night Out

Everyone wears drag round here. The barman
in gold lamé and a vast peroxide wig
serves pints of Sam Smith to a local Carmen

wearing the cruiser's full authentic rig
of white blouse, fish-nets, tiny leather skirt,
with three days' stubble, mouth like a ripe fig.

Richard Roundtree and Jack Palance flirt
in the corner. Norman Hunter and Pat Phoenix
are at their dominoes, quietly talking dirt.

Sniffer Clarke appears after turning tricks
down Harehills, his red handbag open,
orders a drink and prepares to take a fix.

Outside in derelict squares bad things happen,
rapes and stabbings, people are rolling round
in their own vomit, and dark pools deepen

ever deeper, ever darker, moving underground.
Meanwhile the moors are bleak and clear and wild
and the raw north wind is the only keening sound

to haunt or comfort the dreams of a woken child
as hills falls away, an escarpment drops
into place and something grips at roofs recently tiled

and lifts them away from terraces and corner shops
with boarded windows, over garages, towards the sea
where the world grows solemn and everything stops.

Girl Flying

When she stood at the top of the stairs by the door
of the college, the wind caught her up and so
she flew all the way down, as if no more

than a micro-detail on a map that any breeze could blow,
and if she could have flown of her own will
at any time she chose, this was how she'd go,

her coat flapping beneath someone's windowsill,
gone before noted, and the clouds too slopped
from side to side, sliding down some hill

in the distance, too dreamy to be stopped
or even slowed into a world with a clear face
as if suddenly a tiny penny had dropped

about her and everyone else's lack of proper place
in a motorway city above the flyover
with a bird's eye view, but not quite the same grace

as the seagulls she spotted under cloud cover
effing and blinding as she was lifted down,
almost gently, as if to hang or hover

were a privilege, like a silk dressing gown
made of wind she was wearing, whose belt was undone
and as she descended the air it was blown

out like a cord she might pull or the trigger of a gun
which went off the minute she hit the ground
with a dull thud on the surface of the sun.

Poet

He leered softly into his lapel. He listened to the sound
of bells in the distance and turned another page
of his book. It was years since he had found

himself alone like this. There was his image
in the wardrobe mirror, his jacket hung
on the door. It was the passing of an age,

the death of the New Elizabethans, the young
all gone in the air. He reached for the neat gin
in the glass. It slithered sweetly down and stung

his throat, so he filled the glass again.
The cobbled streets outside rang with pity.
It was a lost place and a bad place to begin.

It was James Thompson's notion of the *City
of Dreadful Night*, a night that was creeping up
on him now with alarming alacrity.

The dancing feet of Alexander Pope,
grotesquely blithe, tapped across his brow
in a parody of decorum, hatred and hope.

Too tired to dance with anyone right now.

Chuck Berry Live

Too tired to dance with anyone right now
after the gig, here in the Merrion Centre
where Chuck Berry has just taken his bow

with a riotous, raunchy but disciplined little number
where he mimed the wiping of seed on the wall,
and it was innocent, funny and tender

for the ancient Teds at this ugly bug ball
in their precisely dated costumes of drapes
and winklepickers, their faintly comical

pompadours with bald spots conjuring lost shapes
of threatening baroque splendour down streets
grown dull with rationing, like God's apes

wreaking vengeance for a series of defeats
after the war when fathers disappeared
and came back changed. A steady Leeds rain beats

on Woodhouse Lane creating fountains, weird
rococo pools, washing away the rubbish
with bronze-gold-copper ripples under battered

cars by lamp posts, somehow homely and British,
stabilising into damp, which crawls across
the wallpaper, with old books, silverfish.

Keighley

At night you can see the north wind as you lie
sleepless, because the net curtains bulge
with it, and the whole room seems to sigh

and billow as if the moors were about to divulge
a dreadful secret: black earth, scrub, thin grass.
The weather here is willing to indulge

its resident Heathcliffs from the deep bass
of fogged valleys or screaming tips of rock.
On a bend down Keighley way you might pass

a cannibalised Morris Minor in a state of shock,
its big end gone, its eyesockets picked bare
by scavengers, dewdrops dangling from the lock

of its open door. There is something in the air
stripping the paint away, nature perhaps
nothing more, the power concentrated there

escaping through the bleak beauty that claps
its arms around things, around trees and cars
and old men dropping ash in their own laps

in front of the TV and the latest soap stars,
with the dog by the door wanting to go out
into the wind across the becks and scars.

3 THE PICKETS
(for Terence Brown)

Blockade

Where ideology fails, mere livelihood
takes over, seeking its bottom line,
wherever that is, in vision or in blood

or further regions impossible to define.
The cross of St George flutters on the pole
behind men picketing in a benign

huddle, comfy, but barely in control
of the world that they are bringing into being.
They form a solid yeomanry in droll

revolt against powers that even now are fleeing
the cities they rule from. From what far regions
have the yeoman risen? Where are their all-seeing

leaders and prophets? Their everyday religions
are bottom-line affairs with few demands,
offering basic warmth for mild allegiance,

composed of mostly affordable deodands:
crumbs for the ducks, a tip for the paper-boy,
a Christmas kiss, holding a mother's hands,

comfort for the dying. I'm thinking of Joy,
Ruby, Ted and Jerry, their children trapped
in kitchens and sheds a real storm would destroy

in minutes, and Stan, hollow-eyed, flat-capped,
whose tools we inherited, and Percy Bunn
the handyman and glazier who dropped

dead at the church fête, and gangling Ron
the caretaker, whose wife left and he drank
for weeks, and every picket the son

(or daughter) of people of such social rank
as drop away now, lost in the dawn retreat,
the tankers rolling past them, faces blank.

Orators

The orators came, voting with their feet
and shows of hands. Hands were grasping fags,
clutching and pounding. I remember the discreet

look of the cabinet minister and the bags
under Ron Kosky's eyes as he talked of Paul
Robeson and of the black slaves in their rags.

Thick eyebrows were watching punched cards fall
on office desks. So Gerry Sparks would follow
Frank Chappell to the mighty annual

TUC where Jack Jones laid down the law
(Get your tanks off my lawn, said Callaghan)
while Red Robbo at BL tunnelled away below,

and I was scared of everything: the man
with the power to turn lights off and drop
me back into the chaos where I began

among mobs and bodies, the horde's gallop
towards a single figure which was me
by extension. This was England's shop

with windows broken and nothing inside to see,
and England's work as represented by
estate kids, blokes on buses, Bill and Tubby

in the painter's yard. I would not say
it was a sheltered childhood, but the loud
disturbed me, as did anger and decay.

I was a spectator, watching the crowd
wearing the faces of furious angels: their roar
was me in flames. Soon enough they slowed

back to the daily trudge, the regular shore,
their sea slapping and ebbing, their kind
gestures returning with them to the shop floor

and the parlour and the pub, fags in lined
hands, jokes and telly, the world unaltered,
as if, like me, it feared to be defined.

Orgreave

Out of the dark came the miners. Their villages
were live coals and their bodies fed the flames
that burned their love affairs and marriages.

Black dust coated their tongues and blurred their dreams.
They licked their children into shape like bears
with sore heads. At night they heard the screams

of wheels on tracks or footsteps on the stairs.
They'd rise to the surface and gradually fade
into the morning. They covered their chairs

with rough shadows that left a faint grey tide.
They drank hard and played football with caps for goal-posts,
a few turned out for a professional side

in the nearby town. They prayed for the Lord of Hosts
to lead them into a world of light but woke
at midnight hearing their brothers' ghosts.

Wheels on tracks, collapses. They only needed to poke
the fire for the coals to cave in and bury them deep.
I still remember the day their power broke

at Ollerton, Bidworth, Orgreave. The earth could keep
its darkness. It was the end of the century right now,
the end of the war. A new kind of peace would creep

out of the atom with pale hands, its brow
unlined and vacant. There was something deadly
about its frivolity, which would allow

anything at all except fire and memory.

Scene at a Conference

The kindliness of the English: a paper presented
to the ethnicity conference in Dublin in
2004. The thesis commented

on their slow smiles in a suburban garden
in North London in the early 60s. It cited
a middle-aged hand fingering a pattern

of glossy box-hedge leaves. On being invited
to elaborate, the writer mentioned the old
woman who shyly brought cups of tea to benighted

refugees waiting for a bus one particularly cold
December; three boys in a playground taking
pity on a loner in the doorway who would unfold

an incomprehensible story to them, shaking
with tears; WVS squadrons, patient
bureaucrats at office desks, their heads aching

with figures, and surprisingly efficient
bands of secretaries holding open lines,
all comprehending, almost omniscient.

The constancy of kindliness. The signs
of kindliness on rain-soaked building sites,
in electric sub-stations and down coal mines.

The forms of kindliness: terrible nights
of diffidence in front rooms, quiet
interminable minutes interrupted by flights

of fancy, the unspoken etiquette
of the lower-middle-class tea party; loss
and the coping with; desire within set

limits: all this equated with kindliness.
Warm beer and cricket, mumbled someone
at the back, who had already given his address.

And it was true, there was considerably more fun
at the Gael end of things, at the high table:
charm, invention, a recently fired gun.

Nostalgia

I recall the 70s sliding underfoot
like dead wet leaves. It was perpetual
late autumn, history nibbling at the root

of a gaudy tree. The summer had been lethal.
So many dead and there was no escape
except down cellars. It was the long crawl

to seeming safety that did for us. We lost shape,
shrank back into ourselves, turned minimalist,
steely trimmers, each with a secret tape

of fear. Russia showed us a clenched fist.
Their guns were pointing as were everyone's.
The world was tired. It would not be missed

by bodies in car-boots, fingers pressing buttons.
I don't think we were doing retro then
but who can tell? Shirley had bought patterns

from a stall on the Friday market. There were women
rummaging among hats, cheap scarves and rolls
of cotton, terylene and other off-cuts. When

did this stop, if it has? And those armfuls
of Mills and Boon in the corner? When did they
switch to Black Lace, dream-catchers and lentils?

Some decades age faster than others. We replay
them like old movies. The pickets flying high
over a ruined industrial estate have flown away

into the grey cancer-ridden darkness to die.
And these men are like a flock of starlings
briefly gathered by the refinery

now risen and gone with a lazy flap of wings.

4 ENTERTAINMENTS
(for Brendan Kennelly)

Offence

The yob in the corner with the t-shirt is laughing
at an air disaster in France. The others plead
with him to stop, but there is absolutely nothing

they can do. He's pissed, raw, gone to seed,
knackered, flushed, buggered, all done in.
You can see his head beginning to bleed

with some corrosive liquid. He's about to chin
the man beside him, picks on a girl by the bar
and tells her to suck on this. The others grin,

embarrassed and try containment. He's too far
gone, in a rusty backyard of wires and knives
he can't escape, speaking the innate vernacular

of the trapped. He's shit. Scum. He survives.
But the girl and his mates are watching him drown
in his own mire, like distant relatives

at a death-bed scene. It's a night on the town,
not even a weekend. A gallery next door
shows a drawing of sleek cars sweeping down

steep shadowed streets, a dream or metaphor
or memory of a film where people chase
each other because they're compelled to. The floor

of the pub rears up. Air hits him in the face
like a great cold wave that almost flattens him.
He is the doomed prince, king of infinite space.

The Wrestling

The Corn Exchange is a gaunt railway hall
in the Balkans. Three rows of sundry chairs
at each side of the ring are set out as usual

but you can sit on tables like other punters.
A man or woman with a face quite fallen in,
entirely without teeth; three obese mothers

with fat children; rows of elderly women
in cardigans; a bus driver, a pair
so dense with studs (a rough-cast Pearly Queen

and a King Cobra) they almost buckle
under the weight. And stolid oldies, wise
to the ways of the game, quite as fantastical

as the wrestlers themselves, their heads topiaries
or billiard balls, who know the throws and holds,
have known them for years. The strange cries

of birds, a jungle chattering, the piercing scolds
of angry deities. Anyone not from here
is hated with a pantomime fury. Scaffolds,

hanging-trees, iron maidens, objects of fear.
Two fat leotards, one in a Union Jack,
the other in glitzy blue, engage. The gods appear

and watch them with hooded eyes. Bones crack.
Pantomime turns music hall. It's Marie Lloyd
and the Great War making a belated come back,

a forlorn intimacy crawling from the void,
its grossness sweet and almost delicate,
like love between the lost and the destroyed

or a face in the blurred gallery, painted by Sickert.
The human need for blood, bone, gristle, flesh:
for Justice with her scales and lottery ticket.

Warhol's Dog

Fifteen minutes, and then another fifteen…
like being licked all over by a friendly mastiff.
You are bathed in the light of the television screen,

that slobbers enthusiastically, as if
it loved you, but you are becoming a dog
yourself, with a dog's appetites. You sniff

your way around the world, a mere cog
in the doggy universe, pleased with your place.
You watch doggy programmes, your doggy bag

in front of you, your fixed dog's-grimace
perfect in profile. You are John Bull's cur
and proud of it. Your home is your palace.

Cilla dog makes puppy love happen. Her
little yelps are blessings. Kilroy-Silk
rolls over on his back as if about to purr

then remembers he's a dog. It is the milk
of human kindness running in his veins.
Dogs know one another, recognise their ilk

immediately. Mongrel celebrity rains
cats and dogs. I have seen the chairs turned
to the telly in nursing homes. No one complains.

And when the last doggy remains are burned
in the pet crematorium you may be sure
it will be live. It is what dogs have earned

with their fidelity: a fiery erasure,
a substitute of burning glass. The dog
by the iconic hearth, framed to endure.

The Full Monty

Hen night entails low laughter down at base.
It starts below and rises like a whale
to spout from the fair middle of your face.

It's in your face, it's gone right off the scale.
Your kid is waving it in front of you.
You get it fresh before it all goes stale.

And stale it must go, nothing you can do.
That's why you laugh, to keep it fresh just when
it's started to go off. It's Danish Blue,

it's down there where you need it, where the men
can't see or reach, that source, the tickled zone.
Cheese is what you would say, but you're a hen,

and laughter's brittle as a chicken bone.
Men have no dignity, they have no grace:
without their power they're comical alone,

their nakedness is naked in your face.
No hiding place, just giggles, you're all mates.
Hen night entails low laughter down at base.

Preston North End

Tottenham Hotspur versus Preston North End.
Finney's last season: my first. And my dad
with me. How surprisingly well we blend

with these others. Then the English had
the advantage, but today we feel
their fury, sadness and pity. There were some bad

years in between, a lot of down-at-heel
meandering. For me though, the deep blue
of Preston was ravishment of a more genteel,

poetic kind. They were thrashed 5-1, it's true,
and Finney was crocked by Mackay. Preston went down,
hardly to rise again. But something got through

about Finney the plumber, Lancashire, the Crown,
and those new days a-coming. The crowd dissolves,
but we are of the crowd, heading into town

under sodium street lights. This year Wolves
will win the title. Then Burnley. I will see
Charlton, Law and George Best. The world revolves

around them and those voices on TV
reading the results. I'm being bedded in –
to what kind of soil remains a mystery,

but I sense it in my marrow like a thin
drift of salt blown off the strand. I am
an Englishman, wanting England to win.

I pass the Tebbitt test. I am Allan Lamb,
Greg Rusedski, Viv Anderson, the boy
from the corner shop, Solskjaer and Jaap Stam.

I feel no sense of distance when the tannoy
plays Jerusalem, Rule Britannia or the National Anthem.
I know King Priam. I have lived in Troy.

(for Gerald Morgan)

Death by Meteor

The night the meteor struck, the headline writers
were raising point sizes. The ten o'clock news
was brought forward an hour. In restaurants, waiters

ran from table to table. Theatre queues
were issued with free tickets. England was there
for the taking with Scotland and Wales. The pews

remained empty. Too late now for hot air.
This would be phlegmatic, immediate,
dignified, business as usual. Trafalgar Square

was full of pigeons. Trains would run extra late
until the shadow thickened sometime towards dawn
when the noise would be deafening. So they would wait

in streets or in pubs or on the well-kept lawn
of the bowling green, some tanked up with beer,
others with mugs of tea, some of them drawn

to familiar places, others steering clear
of all acquaintance. An Englishman's home
was the castle at the end of a frail pier,

the silence of a haunted aerodrome
where ghosts were running forward into fire.
Already they could hear the distant boom

of the approaching rock over Yorkshire,
the Midlands, Derby and Birmingham
the pitch rising, ever sharper and higher.

Death by Power Cut

So one by one the fridge, the TV, the iron,
the radio, flickered, shuddered, and went out.
Nobody lit a candle. Not a siren

was heard, just cold and darkness and doubt
leaking away, becoming certainty,
like a hangover after a dizzying bout

of drinking, or a desire for terminal sobriety.
Out went the shop windows. Safeways, Tescos,
McDonalds, Boots, Woolworths, the charity

stores, wine bars, offices, gyms, discos
and restaurants. It was the British winter
closing in for ever. Soon water froze

in the taps and the last of the cheery banter
died away. And the sea grew silent, the sky
fell like a pane of glass, one enormous splinter

of light, and broke across water. Not a cry
escaped their lips. They were proud in defeat.
They were a thirties movie and prepared to die

in black and white if need be, modest and discreet
as their fabled ancestors, thinking in
clipped tones. Then came a flurry of snow and sleet

that covered pavements up with dense white skin.
Lovers moved apart, as if afraid
of what touch might do. The old would grin

and bear it. It was their finest hour. It weighed
on them like history. The darkness blossomed
in them. It was like moving into the shade.

Death by Deluge

I have seen roads come to a full stop in mid-
sentence as if their meaning had fallen off
the world. And this is what happened, what meaning did

that day in August. The North Sea had been rough
and rising and the bells of Dunwich rang
through all of Suffolk. One wipe of its cuff

down cliffs and in they went, leaving birds to hang
puzzled in the air, their nests gone. Enormous
tides ran from Southend to Cromer. They swung

north and south at once, as if with a clear purpose,
thrusting through Lincolnshire, and at a rush
drowning Sleaford, Newark, leaving no house

uncovered. Nothing remained of The Wash
but water. Peterborough, Ely, March, and Cambridge
were followed by Royston, Stevenage, the lush

grass of Shaw's Corner. Not a single ridge
remained. The Thames Valley filled to the brim
and London Clay swallowed Wapping and Greenwich.

Then west, roaring and boiling. A rapid skim
of Hampshire and Dorset, then the peninsula:
Paignton, Plymouth, Lyme, Land's End. A slim

line of high hills held out but all was water-colour,
the pure English medium, intended for sky, cloud,
and sea. Less earth than you could shift with a spatula.

Death by Suicide

It began with the young men. They lost touch
with something important almost as soon as words
entered their mouths. There was not very much

they could say with them. They ambled in herds
like sick cattle, bumping into the edges
of the world. People were sorry afterwards

though some were glad. They leapt off ledges,
drugged themselves, spun from light-cords, drew
knives across their necks. Their very bandages

were infected and their mothers knew
in odd dark moods that they were bound by fate
to join them. And so it spread, steadily through

the whole island, until it was too late.
Life had thinned to a fragile carapace,
bones turned to cartilage. There was a spate

of immolations in the Fens, a case
of hanging-fever in Derby and a bus-load
of climbers cut their own ropes on the rock-face

at Malham. Whole families buckled. Death strode
through darkened living rooms where the radio
droned on, taking possession of one road

after another. Everywhere the sound of low
weeping. Some said it was mere melancholy –
you only had to listen to Elgar, the cello

concerto, to hear the national *folie
de grandeur*: all that aggression dressed
as modesty. Meanwhile the race was busily

killing itself, the sun was sinking in the west,
and one could read the experts' eyes, which were
distinctly bleary. They too were depressed.

The Three Remaining Horsemen of the Apocalypse

Then Fire, Famine, Plague, or what you will
(there was no energy left for War by then)
had drawn their horses up on a high hill

overlooking the city, to observe the men
and women below them. The air hung like ice.
The place had nothing to lose. They saw the pattern

of the everyday squeezed into one brilliant slice
of light. To them, each day sat somewhere
between desire and fear. Their paradise

comprised mere moments. A man in an armchair
was doing the crossword. A woman in a housecoat
was working at her window-box, her hair

gently fluttering across her exposed throat.
Two children were kicking a bottle. A dog ran down
an alley. The whole country seemed to float

like a vast web, unattached. They stood on the crown
of the hill and considered the course of history.
They watched as she progressed with a deep frown

along the river like Cleopatra, feeling sorry
for herself. I myself stared at the wall
of the yard trying to recall the memory

of other days like this. And then a miracle.
Time stopped and was redeemed in the faint
sunlight, the sun hazy, perfectly spherical.